Return to GOLD COUNTRY

John Gilbert

blue7ink

Blue 7 Ink
5268 Lakewood Road
Duluth, Minnesota 558804
www.jgilbert.duluth.com

Return to Gold Country: Minnesota reclaims lost NCAA hockey glory

Copyright © 2002 by John Gilbert. All rights reserved. Except for short excerpts for review purposes, no part of this book may be reproduced or transmitted in any form by any means without written permission from the publisher.

Text and photos by John Gilbert
Copy editing by Joan Gilbert
Cover design and interior layout & design by Tony Dierckins

Photos of players on pages 21–24 are courtesy of the University of Minnesota

02   03   04   05   06   5   4   3   2   1

Publishing Consultation and Production by X-communication
218-724-2095 • www.x-communication.org

Acknowledgements

For the inspiration to try to chronicle the University of Minnesota's surge to the 2001-2002 NCAA men's hockey championship, the author would like to thank the following:

- Every player on the championship team, who blended together to take up a position next to the 1974, 1976 and 1979 NCAA title teams. But also to every player who ever pulled on a Gopher hockey jersey, especially those who played since the 1960s, when I first started realizing that watching the Gophers was watching something special, year after year.

- All the coaches who have gathered together those players, particularly those whose teams I've covered, from John Mariucci, Glen Sonmor, Herb Brooks, Brad Buetow and Doug Woog, to Don Lucia.

- Countless friends and hockey fans from all across the state of Minnesota, and elsewhere, who always fill places like Mariucci Arena with wonderful noise, and who have provided no less support through the years to the words and passion of a reporter who grew older—but not up—in their midst.

- My dad, Wally Gilbert, whose too-short life caused me to love sports forever.... My mom, Mary, who helped me learn to love putting words together. At age 99, unable to see anymore, she made me promise to read this book to her.... My wife Joan, whose support and opinions matter so much that I asked her to edit this book. The only time I was able to "edit" Joan was when I coached her women's hockey team for a year.... My sons, Jack and Jeff, who taught me more than they'll ever know in all those days when I thought I was teaching them something. I coached Jack and Jeff in their formative years of hockey, among other sports, and they cannot comprehend the endless joy they have created in my soul.

- And anyone who gets even a moment's enjoyment from this book.

Contents

Introduction vi
1. Leave a message… 1
2. The cast of characters 7
3. "Inevitable" championship 25
4. Into the modern era 29
5. Those title years 35
6. Coming up short 43
7. Lucia always a winner 47
8. Growing up with expectations 51
9. The transition to "team" 55
10. Teenagers grow up fast 61
11. Change overdue 67
12. Angell finishes on high 73
13. Four great years 79
14. The puck stops here! 85
15. The Pohl chronicles 93
16. Preview of payback 97
17. Only an exhibition 103
18. Season starts fast 109
19. Off-again, on-again 113
20. Gophers finish regular season 127
21. WCHA playoffs 133
22. WCHA Final Five 135
23. Lucia's regional plan 143
24. At home in St. Paul 149
25. Hauser tames the Wolverines 151
26. All-Minnesota, but one 155
27. Getting ready 161
28. Sudden end to classic final 167
29. Two enormous goals 173
30. Golden afterglow 179

Introduction

Growing up a few miles up the North Shore from Duluth, I was able to ride to work with my mother every morning of summer vacation, and get off at Portman Square in Lakeside, where I would try to coax other kids to play baseball, from 7:30 a.m. until 5 p.m. Once school started, that wasn't possible, so I didn't grow up playing hockey. I'd go to Portman, six miles away, on winter weekends once in a while, but I was exiled to the recreation rink, where you could skate only counterclockwise, while my baseball buddies were encased inside these odd boards, skating like crazy after a weird little black disc and occasionally pounding each other's padded bodies.

My dad was Duluth's—and maybe the state's—greatest athlete ever. His name was Wally Gilbert, and he played an incredible sports career at Valparaiso and then in the pros before coming back home to marry my mom. He played third base for the Brooklyn Dodgers and Cincinnati Reds in Major League baseball back in the early 1930s, and he also played pro football for the Duluth Eskimos at the same time, as a fullback, runner, passer, drop-kicker and punter of legendary ability. He also played on a touring semi-pro basketball team out of Two Harbors in those days. And he was a championship curler. He was disabled from a fouled-up surgery for an abscessed lung while working at the Duluth steel plant during World War II, just about the time I was born, and he died when I was a junior in high school. He used to enjoy mingling with old friends at the Duluth Curling Club, and I'd look forward to going with him. But usually I would run upstairs—upstairs!—and watch some hockey game or another, always with great fascination. I can still recall the smell and sound of that creaky upstairs Curling Club rink, with its tiny ice sheet, and the hot water radiators in the lobby.

It was there, in high school, that I watched my Duluth Central classmates on the hockey team upset my summertime baseball buddies from Duluth East in 1960—a year that East won the state title. I played baseball, but if I could have turned right on skates, I'd have been on that hockey team, too. Then I went to the University of Minnesota-Duluth, where the Bulldogs dominated MIAC hockey and were building toward a move to Division One. They had some awesome teams, and the highlights were games against Michigan Tech, North Dakota – and, of course, the University of Minnesota. I loved baseball, and I still play senior men's baseball, and I follow every sport closely as a sportswriter, but even then, I couldn't imagine how any sport could be as fast, as exciting, as spontaneously unpredictable as hockey.

After transfering to Minnesota to study journalism, I attended a state tournament in person, and I followed John Mariucci's Gophers, and I was hooked for life. For the next 35 years, at the *Duluth News-Tribune*, at the *Minneapolis Tribune* and *Star-Tribune*, and briefly for the Murphy McGinnis Newspaper network, I covered every level of hockey. The pros, the colleges, the Olympics, the high schools, kid hockey, and later girls and women's hockey—you name it, I was probably at the game.

I was always fascinated by the success teams had when they played differently. Then I saw the old Soviet Union teams, and was astonished at their puck-control style, compared to the old NHL teams. Same with the Swedes, Finns and Czechs. Then along comes Herb Brooks, having played those teams in international hockey, and he invents his own style of play, something he called "sophisticated pond hockey." He put elements of it to work while he was coaching the Gophers for seven years, and he won three NCAA championships doing various inventive stages of his hybrid style.

From what I learned of the tactics, I had a memorable time coaching both my sons in youth hockey. They are clever, skilled hockey players. When I first went outside with them, I couldn't believe the thrill of gliding across an outdoor rink, managing somehow to control the puck. My wife, Joan, took up the game with some friends when their sons' shinpads got big enough to fit them, and later they got into a high-test league in the Twin Cities. Our younger son, Jeff, is 10 years younger than Jack, which gave us time to enjoy both of them through youth and high school sports. I coached youth hockey teams and tried some of those tactical things, and they worked! I was thrilled, and I realized that you can always learn new things about the game of hockey, as long as you don't decide you know it all.

From those years, I also learned that the most pleasure anyone can get from the sport is to go outside. Our whole family would play 2-on-2 until we could gather assorted other kids from the neighborhood and join in a spirited pickup game. I was just about at Peewee level by the time I was 40. As long as I didn't have to turn to my right.

Through it all, I was honored to cover the 1980 Olympic hockey tournament at Lake Placid, and the North Stars and Fighting Saints in their greatest—and worst—seasons, along with every state high school tournament since 1965, and college hockey. There may be nothing better than high school hockey, at its purist, but no matter which level you prefer, there is something undeniably special about the cult following of the University of Minnesota Golden Gophers. As people gathered to watch their homestate kids take on the college hockey world, they generated an atmosphere that was electrifying.

The passion with which people followed the Gophers spread throughout the state, and every kid in Minnesota who picked up a hockey stick dreamed of someday playing for the Gophers. A few of them made it, and the magic would be extended through another generation. Capturing the whole scene, and writing about it, is a unique experience that I've always cherished. After moving back to Duluth a couple years ago, I stayed close to college hockey, although I wasn't able to stay as close to the 2001-02 Gophers as I would have liked. I covered them at various stages of the season, and all through their WCHA and NCAA playoff run, and then it hit me. I had the time, and as perhaps the only person who had covered all four Gopher NCAA championship teams, I had the perspective. The opportunity to gather together the heroes of the 2001-2002 championship team and let them chronicle their magical season themselves, while I could filter it through the historical perspective, is a perfect way to tell the latest part of the epic story of Gopher hockey.

— John Gilbert, October, 2002

Chapter 1

Leave a message...

ALONG ABOUT THE MIDDLE OF APRIL OF 2002, if you called a certain Southeast Minneapolis apartment, you might hear the answering machine buzz to life. After the usual salutation about nobody being home to take the call, the recorder would say: *"If you want to leave a message for the guy who scored the winning goal in the NCAA Hockey Tournament championship game, press 1.... If you want to leave a message for the guy who scored the tying goal, press 2.... If you want to leave a message for the Hobey Baker Award winner, press 3.... Or if you just want to talk to Troy, press 4."*

What a house! It wasn't an all-star gathering so much as a random gathering, just a coincidental household of eager athletes, part of the gang that came together to secure the University of Minnesota's first national hockey championship in 23 years. It took a long time to return to the pinnacle, but it almost seemed worth the wait, the way this title came about.

The answering machine message started out properly honoring Grant Potulny, the only non-Minnesotan on the roster. He scored the winning goal in the NCAA final on a power play to subdue Maine 4-3 in sudden-death overtime, which wasn't so "sudden" after 16 minutes and 58 seconds had elapsed.

The message also honored Matt Koalska, who was in the midst of having a brilliantly effective game and thus earned the right to be the extra man on the ice with the goalie pulled at the end of the third period. He drilled a shot from the slot for an unlikely goal with 53 seconds remaining—"52.4," Koalska corrected. That goal rescued the Gophers from the all-too-familiar jaws of defeat and forced overtime.

The third player honored by the message was, of course, Jordan Leopold, the buttery-smooth defenseman who was an All-American and had just won the Hobey Baker Memorial Award as the player declared the best in the country.

The only thing about the message that was questionable was that it was sort of an insult to Troy Riddle, the fourth member of the household. He deserved some recognition on the voice message as well, after having assisted on two goals in the title game. It wasn't an insult, after all, because it was Riddle who made the recording, and he chose good humor and the chance to be humble. Maybe that, too, tells a lot about this championship team.

The collection of former high school stars who gathered together to reinstate the University of Minnesota at the top of the NCAA heap in hockey in 2002—the first Gopher hockey title since 1979—consisted of some clever, quick-witted characters wearing the big "M" on their jerseys. But, just like the voice message, any tendencies toward being a hot dog were flushed away in the consuming unity of a true team effort.

"The biggest reason, to me, that we won this year, was that we had great kids," said coach Don Lucia, who struck gold in only his third year of rebuilding the program. "Our best players were great kids. We had great people, with a great work ethic, and they had such respect.

"I mean, how can you not respect Jordan and Johnny?" added Lucia, naming Jordan Leopold and Johnny Pohl, the team's on-ice, off-ice, inspirational and dressing room leaders. "They had everybody's respect because they were extremely hard-working; they were good in school, and good citizens. They're everything you want in a college athlete."

This was a group that pulled together, on and off the ice, as closely knit as some recent previous teams were scattered. And it was that unity, cultivated and nurtured carefully for three years by coach Don Lucia and his staff, and executed by the players themselves, that was as important as any other element in the ultimate championship.

Lucia, who had never won a title while coaching some magnificent teams at Colorado College, nonetheless learned how and why teams that conquered his CC teams did manage to win, and some of the theories he developed over those years became important tools of guidance, also a big part of the championship. He also is first to point out that no matter how carefully you plan and prepare, recruit and coordinate, you can't guarantee a championship. You can only maneuver a group of athletes into position where they have a legitimate shot at ultimate success. The rest is up to them, and to Lady Luck.

"At the start of the season, I thought we were good enough to have a shot at it," said Lucia. "I've always felt that every year, seven or eight teams seem to have a shot to win the national title. Going into the season, I looked at Michigan and Michigan State, because you always look at them, and in our league, Colorado College and St. Cloud figured to be very good, and I thought we were in there. And I thought Denver would be 'way better, but I didn't anticipate they'd be as good as they turned out to be. So, realistically, there were four teams in our league that had a shot at the national title this year.

"Going through it seven times, I feel I've had three teams that were capable of winning the national title," Lucia added. "The 1996 CC team, which lost in overtime to Michigan (3-2) in Cincinnati, that was a great team. We were a little thin on 'D' and Michigan had a great team—half their team went on to play in the National Hockey League. In my last year at CC (1998-99), I also thought we had a legitimate shot. But Derrin Clark broke his arm and Toby Petersen broke his leg, so that wiped out any chance we had, and we lost to Michigan State. Had those two been there, that team was good enough to win it.

"This team was the third team I've coached that I thought was good enough, but there are a lot of questions. Are you going to be healthy? Are your top-end guys going to play, and play their best? You have to be good, and you have to be lucky. You have to get a good draw. You can be a good team and get a bad draw and you're S.O.L.

"We might have had a bad draw this year if we'd beaten Denver in the last game of the WCHA Final Five. We were better off losing that game. As it turned out, losing that game was the best thing that happened to us, because by losing, we got the No. 2 seed West, and that meant we got to play CC on neutral ice. But had we beaten Denver in the WCHA Final Five, we'd have gotten the No. 1 West seed and we'd have had to beat Michigan in Ann Arbor. We did it early in the season, but the playoffs are different. I'd rather play CC in Ann Arbor than Michigan in Ann Arbor.

"By winning at Ann Arbor, it meant we played Michigan here, in St. Paul, not in their building. Things kind of broke our way. That's where you have to be good and you have to be lucky. For me, you just want to be where you're knocking on the door, because if you get there enough, sooner or later you get lucky and win one."

The Gophers got it all together, and got very lucky, on that Saturday night, April 6, at Xcel Center. They had taken an early 1-0 lead, and held a 2-1 lead after two periods, even though Maine had surged to take over the pace of the game by then. A pair of Black Bear goals in the third period gave Maine a 3-2 lead with 4:33 remaining in regulation. With Maine outshooting Minnesota 16-9 in that third period, the 3-2 lead looked formidable.

Gopher boosters predominate among the crowd of 19,324 could be excused for saying they'd seen this before. The Gophers had become heartbreakers to their fans every year since they won their last previous championship, in 1979.

But not this time. With an assortment of mottoes and inspirational statements whirling around in their heads, the Gophers got the chance to pull goaltender Adam Hauser for a sixth skater in the final minute of regulation, with a faceoff in the Maine zone. Superstar center Johnny Pohl was out there on the faceoff, with the top offensive threats, and the sixth attacker was Koalska, who had only nine goals all season, but he had been having the game of his life to that point. It got better when he golfed a loose puck from the slot with a one-timer, scoring to get the tie.

From hopeless, the Gopher emotion went directly to overload. Most of them were convinced they would win the game in the final 53 seconds of regulation. That didn't happen, and overtime ensued. The crowd was on the edge of those Xcel Energy Center seats. And what a crowd! The 19,324 fans broke the NCAA record as the largest ever to watch an NCAA tournament game, a record that had just been set and reset two days earlier in the semifinals.

On the first shift of overtime, a Maine player flipped the puck into the corner of the Minnesota zone. Another Black Bear skater, forechecking hard, veered across in front of the goal. Adam Hauser, the Minnesota goaltender, chopped him down flagrantly with his big goal stick, sending him sliding helplessly 35 feet toward the corner. No penalty was called, although some of Hauser's teammates said they held their breath for a moment, fearing the obvious slash would be called. It wasn't. When Hauser did it a second time, his teammates said they were amazed he got away with it again.

So at 15:58 of the scheduled 20-minute overtime, when Maine defenseman Michael Schutte was called for tripping, more than a few in the building expressed surprise. Schutte, seeing an outlet pass from the Minnesota zone heading toward Matt Koalska, stepped up to attempt a center-ice bodycheck. Koalska ducked the full force of the hit, and nearly missed Schutte's check completely, but instead, Lady Luck smiled on the Gophers simultaneously from three sides. First, they hit knee-to-knee, but neither player was injured; second, Koalska was upended, flying to a crash-landing at center ice; and third, referee Steve Piotrowski immediately called Schutte for tripping.

The call would become a source of post-game analysis, discussion, and some controversy, and it will certainly endure to become a prime subject of debate, whenever the game comes up for reminiscence by players, fans and media types. Because penalties are rarely called in overtime, by tradition—forget right or wrong. And Hauser had escaped Piotrowski's whistle not once, but twice, with infractions which, if anything, were more flagrant. But hockey is an unforgiving sport. There is no time to feel any sympathy for an opponent, no apologies, no mulligans. You can't let an opponent up, just as you know that opponent wouldn't feel any sympathy if the roles were reversed.

The Gophers didn't hesitate. They went right back out and scored the game-winner on the power play, exactly one minute after the penalty was called. After a season of slick plays and beautiful goals, this one was something different. More luck. After Johnny Pohl's faceoff, Jordan Leopold cut loose with a shot from the right point that was more of a mishit than a missile. The puck sailed wide to the left of the goal, and plunked a Maine defender right in the midsection. Pohl swung at the puck but didn't get it. A Maine defender swung at it and also misfired. Grant Potulny, though, doesn't miss in those situations, and he didn't miss this time, swatting the elusive puck past goaltender Matt Yeats.

Bedlam followed. The Gophers raced off the bench, hugging and celebrating and piling onto each other in the emotional and spontaneous dance that has become ritual after hockey championships reach an overtime conclusion. The Black Bears lay sprawled, or knelt, or stood—silently and motionlessly—as they measured their disappointment in inverse proportion to the celebration they were forced to watch.

The big crowd stood long and loud, roaring their approval inside the Xcel Energy Center. More of them, back on campus, were about to have some mini-disturbances that earned all sorts of police reaction. But the fans inside the building were notable on their own.

Two days earlier, when Maine beat New Hampshire 7-2, a throng of 19,227 established an NCAA hockey record by breaking the 1998 mark of 18,276, when Michigan beat Boston College 3-2 in overtime at Fleet Center in Boston. A couple of hours after the Maine-UNH crowd left Xcel Energy Center, a crowd of 19,234 refilled it to see the Gophers knock off Michigan 3-2, breaking the record again. On Saturday, even that standard fell, when the 19,324 filled every crevice in the flashy new arena, raising the three-game total to 57,957.

Obviously, the total was an NCAA record. The championship game crowd broke several records—as the largest NCAA tournament crowd ever, the largest crowd ever to watch the Gophers, the largest crowd ever at Xcel Energy Center, and the largest crowd ever to watch any hockey game in the state of Minnesota. Thousands more around the state and the country watched the final on ESPN cable television.

Previously, the largest Gopher hockey crowd had been 18,523, recorded three weeks earlier in the WCHA Final Five at the same Xcel Center, when Minnesota beat St. Cloud State 3-0. The largest previous crowd at Xcel Energy Center before the 2002 NCAA tournament was 19,042, set when the first-year Minnesota Wild played the Dallas Stars on November 25, 2001.

Not bad for a two-year-old facility that lists a capacity of 18,604. The entire NCAA tournament's Frozen Four was sold out before the 2001-02 season even started, so a record might have been anticipated, even though three straight 19,000-plus gatherings still would have seemed excessive. Either college hockey fans throughout the region were eager to get tickets for what they knew would be entertaining hockey, or maybe the many Gopher loyalists knew, as one of the team's various slogans claimed: "This is our time."

After four years, goaltender Adam Hauser truly spread his wings to lead the Gophers past Maine in the NCAA championship game at Xcel Energy Center.

Chapter 2

The cast of characters

COACH DON LUCIA MAY HAVE BEEN THE ARCHITECT, but he properly gave credit to his players who made the championship run happen. Ego notwithstanding, no matter how prominent the coach, the players still ultimately must score the goals, make the plays, come up with the key saves and put themselves in position to find a way to win games, and a championship. As Lucia explained, about all the coach can do at that point is make sure the fundamentals are in place, then get all the players to pull together, and maybe throw in a few inspirational bits when necessary.

Sometimes players aren't sure what the coaches are thinking, and often the coach has less idea what is going through the minds of his 20-some hockey players. On this Gopher team, the coaching staff and the players seemed to find harmony, and when the coaches put together their final design, none of the players complained. If they had any disagreements, they bypassed them to contribute to the team concept.

"On our group of forwards, everybody had a niche," said Lucia. "They all had roles, and there weren't a lot of people thinking they should be doing something else. I think everybody felt comfortable. You could break down our team. Here are our superstars—guys who were going to score a lot of goals—and here are the guys who will chip in, here are the guys who will kill penalties and here are guys who are going to be good along the wall. On a lot of teams, guys aren't happy with their roles.

"The real strength of this team is that if you look at our top three centers—Johnny Pohl, Jeff Taffe and Matt Koalska—all three are gifted players. John Pohl is a first-team All-American, Taffe scored 34 goals, and Koalska was one of our best players in the tournament play. Johnny Pohl graduates, and Taffe left to sign a pro contract. He'd have been an All-American/Hobey Baker kind of player if he'd have come back."

Taffe was second in the nation in goals with 34, Pohl led the nation in assists with 52 and points with 79 to set a sizzling pace for the talented forwards. But offensive balance was only part of the winning combination.

In the NCAA championship game, the media folks in the Xcel Energy Center press box were given the usual pressbox lineup sheets and background profiles, along with the all-important depth charts, which show how the teams' forward lines and defensive pairings are aligned. Coach Lucia agreed to provide a brief overview about each player, according to the order in which he had positioned them, by line and pairing. What better way to identify the championship Golden Gophers?

FIRST LINE

16 NICK ANTHONY
5-10, 190, JUNIOR LEFT WING FROM FARIBAULT, SHATTUCK-ST. MARY'S HIGH SCHOOL
9 GOALS, 9 ASSISTS—18 POINTS IN 25 GAMES

"Nick played with a broken foot, after he blocked a shot in our first playoff game," Lucia said. "It was a hairline fracture on the top of his foot, and he didn't play in the WCHA Final Five final. He'd been a catalyst for us.

"We thought he had pulled a groin, earlier in the season, and it turned out to be a sports hernia. After they figured it out, he had surgery right after Christmas. He didn't come back until mid-February, and then he scored some real big goals for us. He was a 'top-three-lines' player, but when he came back, he didn't really have a set spot, so he was all over the place, on different lines. He had some third-line roles, and he ended up on the first line. He'll be one of two seniors coming back for 2002-03, and he's so versatile he became kind of a utility guy for us. He's quiet. Never says anything. He can play center or wing, and he's an extremely hard worker. We use Nick on the penalty kills, and 4-on-4. He's one of those guys you have to have to win. He has good quickness, and he's left-handed, so we used him on some key draws."

9 JOHNNY POHL
6-0, 187, SENIOR CENTER FROM RED WING
27-52—79 IN ALL 44 GAMES

"Johnny Pohl is as fine a player as I've ever been around in 22 years of coaching. He is the hardest-working player I've ever coached. As much as anybody, he put the team on his back in January and February and carried us the rest of the way.

"He's a right-handed center, and he was our key faceoff man. He was injured his junior year. He broke his foot, and broke his wrist. He played with a cast on his hand after breaking the navicular bone in his wrist, which hampered his shooting, but not his passing, playmaking, or work ethic.

"He had an All-American year for us, and nobody is prouder than Johnny Pohl to be on that mural of Gopher All-Americans. He was maligned his freshman year, but since I've been here, he's provided great leadership. We pin our hopes on him. I've always given the captains a lot of say, and he's a good reason why. If anything, he always is thinking of the team, even down to passing first and shooting second. How close this team became is a tribute to Johnny Pohl, because he brought the freshmen in and made sure what the chemistry of this team would be.

"He'll get signed by St. Louis, and he'll be a great pro. The only thing better for him might have been if he wouldn't have gotten drafted, because then every team might have wanted him."

21 TROY RIDDLE
5-10, 170, SOPHOMORE RIGHT WING FROM MINNEAPOLIS, BENILDE HIGH SCHOOL
16-31—47 IN 44 GAMES

"We moved Troy up to the line with Pohl after Dan Welch came back. Troy has tremendous speed, and he became a good defensive player. He was on our second power-play unit, and on the penalty kill. He's very good 4-on-4. He has breakaway speed, so we used him with Pohl on the penalty kills.

"He's a hard worker and really takes care of his body. He's made a lot of progress. He has a strong work ethic, and he's really matured. At some point, kids get it, and Troy made the move this season, on the ice. I noticed a jump from his freshman year to his sophomore year. He wanted to get better. He can really shoot, and he's got to work now on finishing a little better, because with his speed he gets so many chances.

"He's one of those guys who played well for us, but has an even better future. It seems like the seniors mean so much, but when they leave, the torch gets passed down, and Troy is one of those guys it will be getting passed to."

SECOND LINE

18 GRANT POTULNY
6-2, 196, SOPHOMORE LEFT WING FROM GRAND FORKS, N.D.
15-19—34 IN 43 GAMES

"He's a great leader. He is a rah-rah guy in the locker room, and he was an assistant captain as a sophomore this year," said Lucia. Potulny was subsequently elected captain as a junior for 2002-03. After graduating from red River High School, he played two years with Lincoln in the USHL.

"He's not the prettiest skater, but he does the job in the corners. He was an older junior guy coming in. Nobody knew him, he had no reputation because he isn't from Minnesota. But he's good around the net and he plays with great character. We didn't look at him as a key player to make the fancy plays, but a key part to keep the motor running.

"Maybe the role-player is the type of player Minnesota hasn't been recruiting. When I looked back at those championship teams, Herbie's teams always had role players who were experienced and tough. As the playoffs come around, there is less space and more battles around the net. In those situations, pretty players are not as effective. And those are Grant's kind of games. He scored six goals for us in four NCAA games."

22 JEFF TAFFE
6-2, 177 JUNIOR CENTER FROM HASTINGS
34-24—58 IN 43 GAMES

"He was the most skilled player on our team, no question about it. The torch got passed from Erik Westrum to Jeff Taffe to score some goals for us this year and he had exactly the type of year we needed. He made it look easy. He has terrific hands.

"It seemed like he scored a big goal every game. He didn't have the five-point nights, but he was very consistent. He probably had the greatest potential on the team out of high school. He had the size, but he was only 155 pounds. He needed to get stronger physically, and he did that, over the last two years. Last summer, the light bulb went off in Jeff's head. He seemed to realize what he had to do become a great player. Jeff worked harder in the off-season.

"I'm really disappointed he left to turn pro, but it's hard to pass up the kind of money Phoenix offered him. Should have been a second-team all-league forward. If he'd come back, next year he'd be the No. 1 forward in the league and a Hobey Baker candidate."

23 DAN WELCH
5-11, 195 SOPHOMORE RIGHT WING FROM HASTINGS
4-7—11 IN 19 GAMES

"We knew that his experience would be a big benefit. He and Doug Meyer had some academic problems as freshmen and they went to play junior while they regained their eligibility. [Meyer transferred to St. Cloud State.] Dan had a good year at Omaha. Last fall, he went to Normandale Community College to get academically ready. He was readmitted, but he couldn't play until the January 24-25 series against Denver. At 195 or 200 pounds, he was good along the wall. He made our lineup better, and he became a good 5-on-5 player.

"We knew he would be a top-three-lines guy, it wasn't like he was a fifth-line guy coming back, and we played him accordingly, on our four lines. But when you get down to playoffs, it's hard to play four lines because there are so many time outs and a lot of special teams play, so you have to make sure you get your best guys on the top three lines. We tried Danny with Troy Riddle and Jeff Taffe, his former high school teammate, and then we moved him up with Johnny Pohl. He was another piece of the puzzle."

THIRD LINE

11 ERIK WENDELL
6-1, 210, SENIOR LEFT WING FROM BROOKLYN CENTER, MAPLE GROVE HIGH SCHOO
8-9—17 IN 44 GAMES

"Erik is another excellent role player. He's good along the wall, and a strong corner guy. At 210 pounds, he's physically very strong. He didn't play any specialty teams for us, but he played that role well where he was going to bang some people, and go to the net hard."

Lucia was asked if an accurate assessment of Erik Wendell might be that he doesn't run the goalie more than once a game, except sometimes.

"It's not like Erik would run into goalies intentionally," Lucia said. "He just went to net hard. He's a great kid, always has a smile on his face, and has a tremendous work ethic, and a big heart. If you're going to be successful, you've got to have some guys like Erik on the team. He's not one of the 'glamour' guys, but one of the guys who do some of the dirty work. He's tough to move. We didn't want Erik to score goals, we just wanted him to play well defensively, make good decisions with the puck, and get it in deep. He wasn't going to come through the neutral zone and fake three guys out. You didn't want the puck on his stick, you wanted him to put his head down and go to the net in the offensive zone, and score off rebounds."

24 MATT KOALSKA
6-0, 195 SOPHOMORE CENTER FROM ST. PAUL, HILL-MURRAY HIGH SCHOOL
10-23—33 IN 44 GAMES

"Mattie is extremely skilled. He's an impact player and he was outstanding at the Frozen Four. You could argue that he was our best player in the Frozen Four. We had a big talk with that line, because we felt if we were going to win it all, that line had to play better than they had at the WCHA Final Five. We felt very comfortable with our top three lines and we didn't care about any matchup with our top three lines against anybody's top line. We were always more worried about matching up our defensemen against the other team's top line. If we had Mattie's line out there against the other team's top line we didn't care, because they were good defensively, and could score with them.

"Mattie really played extremely well and he's so highly skilled. He's a classic example of a guy who played in the USHL, and made himself a better player. He wasn't really highly recruited. If he didn't come here, I think he'd have gone to Mankato.

"The big challenge to Matt was to convince him that he was a good player, and make him mentally strong. He was, by the end."

27 BARRY TALLACKSON
6-4, 196, FRESHMAN RIGHT WING FROM ST. PAUL, JOHNSON HIGH SCHOOL
13-10—23 IN 44 GAMES

"He went from St. Paul Johnson to the Ann Arbor program for two years. He's extremely talented, big and strong, and can shoot the puck a ton. He's very strong defensively. He was on our second power-play unit because he's so good around the net. He killed penalties, because he's very sound defensively. He had 12 or13 goals as a freshman, which is a very good freshman year.

"We thought he might be a late first-round draft pick in the NHL. He's got excellent size, at 6-4 and 200 pounds. We just had to get him playing consistently as the year went on, and he became a very dependable player by the end of the year. With his size, he's also a good skater. And he's very quiet. You see him, but you don't hear him much."

FOURTH LINE

25 PAT O'LEARY
6-2, 203, SENIOR LEFT WING FROM PLYMOUTH, ARMSTRONG HIGH SCHOOL
4-2—6 IN 40 GAMES

"He had been such a big star in his high school career, but Pat was—I don't know if 'content' is the right word—but he did the job we wanted him to do on the fourth line. He had a great attitude. He could have been a senior on the fourth line who was bitter, but Pat was very positive, great on the bench. He was always very encouraging, very positive to his teammates, and never became bitter. He's got very good hands. He was a little passive, and such a big kid. He wasn't the quickest getting out of the blocks, but a good kid. Such a good kid, and kind of a jokester in the locker room, with a good sense of humor."

29 JAKE FLEMING
5-9, 164, FRESHMAN CENTER FROM OSSEO
3-9—12 IN 43 GAMES

"Jake went to Ann Arbor in the USA Development program as a sophomore and junior. He had a birthdate [August 28, 1982] that meant he could only play two years on the national team, so he was too old to play there so he went and played at Omaha in the USHL as a senior in high school. He committed before he went down to Omaha, He's a good two-way centerman. He killed penalties, is smart, and he won some key draws for us.

"We didn't need him to put up numbers offensively, we needed him to play well defensively. He only had something like three goals, but two of them were shorthanded goals. And he was very effective killing penalties for us."

5 JON WAIBEL
5-11, 185, SOPHOMORE RIGHT WING FROM BAUDETTE
5-4—9 IN 44 GAMES

"Jonny played in Ann Arbor for two years. He's a sophomore who played some at center, when we had Koalska playing some wing. He was one of our top three or four penalty killers. He's very good defensively. In the middle of year, and toward the end, he was a guy we wanted on the ice when we were up by a goal. We'd play him at right wing with Johnny Pohl and Jeff Taffe in the closing minute.

"He hasn't developed into a big scorer, but has became a very good defensive, checking-type forward. He could get 10-12 goals, but I'd be surprised if he'd ever be a 20-goal guy. We had the mix. He was valuable for what he could do. At 185 pounds, 5-11 or so, he can run into some people."

Defense was 'best'

Turning to defense, Lucia, a former defenseman himself, didn't hesitate. "I think we had the best defensive corps in the country," he said, flatly.

The Gopher defensemen not only took care of defending the goal in a manner Gopher goaltenders had not been accustomed in recent years, but they were almost always efficient and often brilliant about supplying quick-outlet passes or creative breakout plays that could turn defense to offense with quick-striking attacks. In addition, the players manning the defense slots were a perfect balance of skaters, puck-handlers and shooters, and their ability to move up alertly to join the forwards for fourth-attacker sorties led to many Minnesota goals simply by catching foes off-guard and outnumbering them at their net.

Jordan Leopold, the All-WCHA, two-time All-America and Hobey Baker winner, got the most credit for those multiple-faceted capabilities, but he was not the only member of the Gopher defense that could become downright offensive. Sophomore Paul Martin and freshman Keith Ballard also displayed gifted offensive abilities, with one on each tandem blended with the more defensive styles of Matt DeMarchi, Judd Stevens and Nick Angell.

1ST DEFENSE

3 JORDAN LEOPOLD

6-0, 210, SENIOR LEFT DEFENSEMAN FROM GOLDEN VALLEY, ARMSTRONG HIGH SCHOOL
20-28—48 IN 44 GAMES

"What can you say enough about Jordan?" said Lucia. "A two-time All-American, and Hobey Baker winner.... He made it look easy how he played his position. I can't really compare him to anybody I've had. Mike Crowley probably was a more gifted offensive player here, but Jordan was good both ways, and what Jordan could also do is really shoot a puck. He had 20 goals, which is really unheard of for a collegiate defenseman. He broke the all-time record here for defensemen.

"His strength was getting the puck out of our zone, because he had such a low panic point with the puck. He could always make a good play, even under pressure. And he was great at joining the rush offensively. He wasn't a guy to carry the puck end to end, but once we were in the offensive zone, many times he'd be the late guy coming in. He could shoot and score from the point, but many times he'd move in and score at the top of the circles, or come in on the weak side, between the hash-marks, and score from that area.

"He always had the green light. I told Jordan, 'Hey, when you feel you have an opportunity, go. Do what you do best. Read the play.' I never wanted to handicap the elite offensive players at our level. I've always wanted them to react to things, go make a play."

19 MATT DEMARCHI

6-2, 186 JUNIOR RIGHT DEFENSEMAN FROM BEMIDJI
3-8—11 IN 36 GAMES

"We played Matt with Leopold, and they were the two we always wanted out there against other team's top line. Matt is a tough, stay-at-home complement to Jordan. They worked together well. Matt would get the puck to Jordan, and it would get out of our zone. Matt took some penalties, but at the end, Matt played very well, and with great discipline. One of the things I tried to stress to our 'D' was that in a low-scoring game, there's nothing wrong with flipping it off-the-glass now and then. We don't want to play that way all the time, but late in a game, late in the season....

"The best thing that happened to Matt, was a bad penalty against North Dakota in first round of the league playoffs, with two minutes to go in the game on the second night. North Dakota scored with 17 seconds to go and their goalie pulled, and we had to go into overtime. We ended up winning, but I'm sure when he was in penalty box and they scored, he was thinking about what a bad penalty that was. He didn't take a bad one after that.

"Matt also was good penalty killer, and with his toughness, he brought a lot of good to the table. He helped give Jordan a lot of room and freedom to go. You can't have six guys rushing the puck."

2ND DEFENSE

10 PAUL MARTIN
6-2, 172, SOPHOMORE LEFT DEFENSEMAN FROM ELK RIVER
8-30—38 IN 44 GAMES

"Paul is a treat to watch. You almost have to be a hockey purist to really appreciate all the subtle things he does, and how good he is at it. There was not a better passer on the team. And not a smarter player. He had a great freshman year, and now a great sophomore year. When you needed to get the puck out of our zone, if Paul had the puck, all it took was one pass and you're gone. He's also good defensively, but his best asset is he has terrific, terrific hands.

"I think next year, he'll do more. He was second-fiddle to Jordan, but now with Jordan graduating, the torch gets passed. When we'd be ahead by a goal late in the game, we'd have Jordan, Paul or Matt—two of those three—out there. Maybe Paul's biggest strength is that he has tremendous vision. He's a guy who wants to make every pass tape-to-tape, and if there's anything he might improve on is that if he goes on to someday play in the NHL, you can't make direct passes all the time and sometimes you have to just dump it off the glass to get it out of the zone. On our Olympic rink, he can make all those tape-to-tape passes. That's one of the reasons we wanted to practice at Augsburg before the tournament, so we could adjust to playing on a rink that was 200-by-85, smaller than our Olympic rink, so our defensemen could adjust to facing more contact, where they can't make direct passes.

"Our nemesis all year long as a team was trying to make the perfect play all the time, trying to do too much, and making turnovers. We had to adjust to make sure we got to the other end of the rink, so other teams would have to go 200 feet to beat us. Paul is an artist. He wanted every painting to be beautiful. We had to convince him that there's nothing wrong with a couple of ugly ones. Maybe they're not as valuable to sell, but they can be just as important."

6 JUDD STEVENS

6-1, 193, FRESHMAN RIGHT DEFENSEMAN FROM WAYZATA

1-15—16 IN 41 GAMES

"Judd came directly out of Wayzata High School, although he went before and after his senior year and played a little at Green Bay in the USHL. No question, he exceeded our expectations. During the first half of the year, he played with Keith Ballard on the second power-play unit. He has great hands, and makes very good decisions with the puck.

"As with any freshman, he had to become a better defensive player. His biggest strength is his hands. As a coach, I knew that when the puck was on his stick, he'd make good decisions. I've always liked defensemen who could make plays with the puck. That's a real important element of the game."

3RD DEFENSE

13 KEITH BALLARD

5-11, 196, LEFT DEFENSEMAN FROM BAUDETTE

10-13—23 IN 41 GAMES

"Keith is another one of those defensemen with great offensive instincts," said Lucia. "I've always said I'd rather have too many of them than too few. He scored those numbers without ever playing on the first power play, and the difference in time between the first and second power play units was like night and day. If we didn't have Jordan and Paul, he would have had to do a lot more.

"He's extremely gifted offensively; and could be a riverboat gambler as a freshman at times. I'd rather have him play a little bit lower risk game at times, but his play is still evolving. He didn't move to defense until ninth or tenth grade and was a forward before then. He can shoot it. And he's very competitive. He's got to learn to not be quite so hard on himself. Make some mistakes, skip it and let it go. As an 18-year-old, when he'd make a mistake it would affect him for stretches of the game. We had a good situation for Keith, though, because we had some other gifted offensive defensemen. It was nice for him to walk in and not feel like he had to do it all."

26 NICK ANGELL
6-0, 205, RIGHT DEFENSEMAN FROM DULUTH, EAST HIGH SCHOOL
4-11—15 IN 44 GAMES

"Did you ever see that poster, with the cat hanging by its front claws and the caption, 'Hang in there?' Every team has a kid who needs to have someone putting a foot to his rear end to keep him working. He had a great senior year. He played very well from start to finish, especially the last month or two of the season, when he played his best hockey. We kid around that he could probably win the Tour de France because he spent so much time on the bike to keep his weight down. He was never the quickest guy, but he had the hands and made the plays.

"We made the change late in the season and put Nick back on the power play unit, and he scored some big goals for us. I alternated him with Joey Martin in that spot until Joey got a concussion against Wisconsin. Nick stayed there and scored a goal to put us ahead against CC in the NCAA quarter-final game. Nick gave us a very good senior year. He matured, and he was appreciative of how it worked out. That's the way you want it. All kids mature at different times, and for Nick it happened between his junior and senior years."

Protecting goaltenders

Coach Lucia sought defensemen who would be capable of bolstering the offense, and he let them go right up to the limit of being too eager, then he backed them off at the end of the season.

"That was one of the big things we had to get across to our defensemen late in the season," Lucia said. "Late in games they sometimes still wanted to play that high-risk game. We had to show video clips of how we could get in trouble trying to score one more when we were ahead by a goal or two. That's when we wanted them to stay home. Maybe we changed how the game was played in the last 10 minutes. A couple times, Jordan would hop in when he didn't have to and the play would go the other way, until we got it across to our 'D' to make good decisions and play the percentages.

"Paul Martin does that very well, but sometimes Keith Ballard would need to be cautioned. Even Jordan a couple of times would get caught in, and obviously, I didn't want them to rush in too aggressively with 10 minutes to go in a game where we were already ahead."

But having the ability to do that freely supplied a definite punch to help when the Gophers trailed.

In goal, senior Adam Hauser benefitted by the challenge—and the occasional breaks—provided by freshmen Travis Weber and Justin Johnson, and overcame a four-year accumulation of criticism for team failures, and his own quest for perfection, to finish as the WCHA's all-time leader in games played (151), and—critics be silenced—the most career victories with 83. Ron Grahame, goaltender during Denver's peak of power three decades earlier, had won 82 games. League teams played fewer games in those days, but Denver also won almost all its games during Grahame's tenure. Going into the Frozen Four, Hauser needed one more victory to catch Grahame; he caught him in the semifinals and set the record anew in the final.

GOALTENDERS

1 ADAM HAUSER

6-2, 210, SENIOR GOALIE FROM BOVEY (GREENWAY OF COLERAINE HIGH SCHOOL)
23-6-4, 2.42 GOALS-AGAINST IN 35 GAMES

"Going into the year, Adam had question marks," said Lucia. "Every year he became better, but people still had all these question marks. Early in his career, Adam was 18. Now as senior, he had a bad game at North Dakota, and a bad game at Wisconsin when Jeff Sauer announced his retirement. Those were his only bad games. He still had the question mark in WCHA Final Five, but he beat St. Cloud, then even though we lost the Denver game in the finals, he played fine, but our team didn't play that good.

"So after all the criticism he got, all Adam did was break all the records here, and break the record for most wins in WCHA history. Every year, he became a better goaltender. That's what you're supposed to do in college. Adam won as a sophomore in the playoffs, but his junior year he didn't play well. But you have to go through those games. We lost to Maine last year, but those games are critical to get you to the next level. This year, going into the playoffs, I felt that if Adam stopped 9 of 10 shots, we'd win. He ends up with 2.5 goals-against and a 91 save-percentage, he plays the puck decently, and he had a spectacular Frozen Four.

"Also, I think by not playing as many games this year, Adam became a better teammate. Before, he'd isolate himself every game. This year when he wasn't playing, he'd be playing hacky-sack with the guys."

31 TRAVIS WEBER

5-11, 200, FRESHMAN GOALIE FROM HIBBING
6-2-0, 3.29 GOALS-AGAINST IN 10 GAMES

"Travis left Hibbing High School to play on the USA National Development team, and he was highly recruited. He had knee surgery last year, so he couldn't do anything all summer long. He had to do a little catch-up all summer to get in proper shape, and all year, actually. He got a chance to play some games, and we got exactly what we wanted out of him. Like any 18-year-old goalie, he had some great games, and some bad ones. He showed he could win some important games for us, like at North Dakota, and by beating Denver, so he got to play in some big games."

33 JUSTIN JOHNSON
5-10, 174, FRESHMAN GOALIE FROM HAM LAKE
3-0-0 AND 3.08 GOALS-AGAINST IN 6 GAMES

"I wanted to redshirt Justin, to get him out of the same class as Travis," said Lucia. "But he didn't want to do that. He wanted to get through college and go to grad school, and he's already a 2-year junior player. He, also, had some very good games and a couple bad games. For both those guys, Travis and Justin, it was difficult to get into any rhythm, because they were only playing once every two or three weeks. But Justin went to Grand Forks and played. Now we'll start next year alternating. Both are great kids, both are extremely good team guys, and both have good work ethics. Now it will be their turn, and we'll be able to sit back and watch."

STRENGTH IN RESERVE

20 JOEY MARTIN
6-3, 203, SOPHOMORE DEFENSEMAN FROM ROGERS (BUFFALO HIGH SCHOOL)
0-4—4 IN 11 GAMES

"Joey was our seventh defenseman, and was playing very well until he got a bad concussion at Wisconsin [Feb. 22]. When he went down, his helmet came off and he fell back and the back of his head slammed onto the ice. He went into convulsions, and it was a pretty scary deal. The ambulance came out on the ice and everything. Fortunately, he was all right, but he missed too much time to get back in when we were in the playoffs. I don't think he was really ready to play until about the NCAA tournament.

"He's physical, at 6-3, and 210 or 215 pounds, and probably was the best hitter on our team. Joey makes punishing hits. I played him at fourth-line left wing last year a little so we could have that physical presence on our team."

14 CHAD ROBERG
5-11, 174, JUNIOR WING FROM DULUTH EAST
0-0—0 IN 3 GAMES

"The guys absolutely love him," said Lucia. "He's a phenomenal team guy. He came to me and wanted to try out my first year, and Mike Randolph, his coach at Duluth East, told me what a great kid he was. So I invited him to walk on, and I fell in love with his enthusiasm. Nobody worked harder every day in practice than he did. There were times last year when I threw him in there to jump-start somebody else. Guys love him, wonderful attitude. He almost quit in the first semester of his freshman year, then he got a B or two and got shook up. I liked his attitude so much, I told him he'd always be on the team."

28 BRETT MACKINNON
5-11, 191, FRESHMAN DEFENSEMAN/WING FROM WAYZATA
1-3—4 IN 21 GAMES

"Brett came in as both a forward and defenseman, and ended up playing more at forward. He's older, having played two years at Cedar Rapids in the USHL after graduating from high school. He's more mature, physically strong, smart, and a good skater. He played quite a few games, and we think he can be a good player for us. He was a great fourth line guy for us this year, and played with energy. For the last year and a half of junior he played more defense, and at 5-10 and 190, he's real strong. One of those kids who will go through the wall for you. McKinnon played in WCHA Final Five but got hurt. He sprained his ankle real bad in the Denver game and couldn't play.

15 MIKE ERICKSON
6-2, 186, FRESHMAN FORWARD FROM EDEN PRAIRIE
1-2—3 IN 9 GAMES

"If Mike would have been healthy, he definitely would have played regularly. He scored the team's first goal in his first game, our exhibition opener at North Dakota. Just when he seemed to get into the rhythm of what's required at this level, he got hurt in the Duluth series in mid-November. He broke a bone in his foot and had to have surgery. It turned out, he played one too many games to qualify for a redshirt year."

17 GARRETT SMAAGAARD
5-11, 167, FRESHMAN WING FROM EDEN PRAIRIE
1-2—3 IN 19 GAMES

"He blew out his knee, and had major surgery on his ACL, in the football championship game and sat out his whole last year of high school hockey," said Lucia. "I wanted him to go play junior this year, but he didn't want to. Garrett played in some games, but he just needs more time to come back after missing an entire season."

First Line

16 Nick Anthony

9 Johnny Pohl

21 Troy Riddle

Second Line

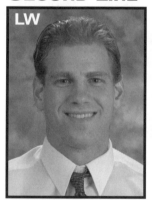
18 Grant Potulny

22 Jeff Taffe

23 Dan Welch

Third Line

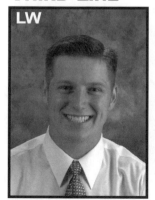
11 Erik Wendel

24 Matt Koalska

27 Barry Tallackson

Fourth Line

25 Pat O'Leary   29 Jake Fleming   5 Jon Waibel

First Defense

 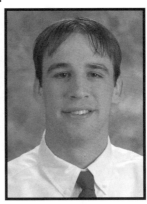

3 Jordan Leopold   19 Matt DeMarchi

Second Defense

10 Paul Martin   6 Judd Stevens

THIRD DEFENSE

13 KEITH BALLARD

26 NICK ANGELL

GOALTENDERS

1 ADAM HAUSER

31 TRAVIS WEBER

33 JUSTIN JOHNSON

Reserves

28 Brett MacKinnon

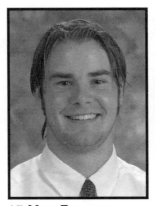
15 Mike Erickson

17 Garrett Smaagaard

20 Joey Martin

14 Chad Roberg

Coach

Coach Don Lucia

Chapter 3

'Inevitable' championship

EVER SINCE 1979, it was inevitable, if you asked anyone who ever paid attention to the University of Minnesota's hockey program. Every year, the inevitability of another Gopher national championship was the primary subject of hockey fans throughout the long Minnesota winters. "This" would be the year that the Gophers would go all the way.

That inevitability was first outlined back in the '70s, when Herb Brooks coached the Gophers for seven years, and captured three NCAA championships in that brief excursion through the Minnesota sports history books. The building blocks had been first laid by the legendary John Mariucci, who coached Brooks as a player, and by the colorful Glen Sonmor, who took Brooks on as an assistant. But while establishing the Minnesota program as a focal point for homestate players, the 20 teams coached by Maroosh and Sonmor through the 1950s and into the 1970s never won an NCAA title.

Mariucci's teams peaked in the '50s, when the incomparable Johnny Mayasich led the way, and the small cult-like number of college hockey teams met for a championship in Colorado Springs every year. But the 1953 Minnesota team lost 7-3 to Michigan in the national final, and in 1954 a heavily-favored Gopher team gave up the tying goal with 1:42 left and was upset by Rennselaer Polytechnic Institute in a 5-4 heartbreaker.

Under Sonmor, the Gophers lured regular capacity crowds to the old Williams Arena and captured a spectacular WCHA championship in 1970, led by the brilliant goaltending of Murray McLachlan and a feisty, irrepressible freshman named Mike Antonovich. The next year, with McLachlan graduated, Antonovich again led the way from a shaky start to the NCAA Final Four in Syracuse, N.Y., where the Gophers rallied from behind to beat

Harvard 6-5 in a semifinal thriller. But in that 1971 title game, Minnesota fell 4-2 to Boston University.

Those teams established some serious ground-rules for the future, but it wasn't until Brooks took over that the Gophers struck gold. In 1971-72, Sonmor left in midseason to organize the Minnesota Fighting Saints of the old World Hockey Association. Ken Yackel, another former Gopher legend, took over as interim coach, then insisted his old friend, athletic director Paul Giel, should hire Brooks.

Giel made the move, and Brooks put the pieces of an 8-24-0 record back together to lift Minnesota up to 15-16-3 overall and 12-13-3 in the WCHA. It was a big step, but nobody realized exactly how big until the following year, which was the 1973-74 season.

In that season, only the second year of Brooks's tenure, the Gophers won their first NCAA championship. They won in 1976, also. And they won in 1979 with a team that would, under Brooks, become the nucleus for the 1980 Miracle on Ice gold medal Olympic champions at Lake Placid.

Surely titles and trophies would follow with similar regularity. Everyone was certain of that, whether media, or fans, or cynics, or foes, or Gopher players past, present and future. But it didn't happen. Brad Buetow followed Brooks as coach for the next six years, then Doug Woog took the helm for 14 years, and while both of them had strong teams—and occasionally sensational teams—the Gophers repeatedly got close but fell short.

Ten years passed, then 15, and then 20 years, and by the time the 2001-2002 season was about to start, 22 seasons of futility had slipped past. The Gophers—still the Golden Gophers to their ever-expanding public relations staff—had long since moved into one of the finest hockey facilities in the world, and drew record crowds while bringing record financial success to Mariucci Arena. But the terms "national championship" and "Gophers"—to say nothing of "inevitable"—were no longer compatible in the same sentence.

All of which made it so much sweeter when what used to be called "*Gopherhockey*" again became truly Golden, gathering all sorts of disparate elements for an act that came together at precisely the right time to win the 2002 NCAA championship in the Frozen Four tournament at the Xcel Energy Center in Saint Paul.

The ingredients were many and varied. Coach Don Lucia, who became the first non-M-Man in modern history to coach the Gophers when he replaced Doug Woog in 1999, spent two years adjusting to the circumstances he found. The once-proud program had slipped from the ranks of the nation's elite hockey teams, despite continued financial success, and was scattered in its style and team functionality. In Lucia's first year, he found how much adjustment would be required, and he also found a splendid crop of sophomores who could be the nucleus to carry off that adjustment to success. They had shown great character by surviving a freshman season that was rugged and frustrating, and the character ingrained in those freshmen remained a beacon that could lead to complete team unity three years later, when they were seniors.

That heart-and-soul group of seniors in 2001-02 was the baseline from which Lucia could build a team to his personal standards of unified performance. The six seniors were split among three high-profile standouts who commanded the headlines as much as they commanded the complete respect of their teammates and foes alike—Johnny Pohl up front, Jordan Leopold on defense and Adam Hauser in goal. No less important to the team success were the three other willing and eager senior contributors—forwards Erik Wendell and Pat O'Leary and defenseman Nick Angell—whose competitive zeal made them perfect ingredients in the drive for team success, regardless of personal achievement.

With that group of seniors establishing the highest of team-oriented standards, from freshmen to veterans, Lucia paused in his quest to have all the ingredients in place and looked wisely to the past as a means to achieve the future with his present team. He studied those Herb Brooks teams from the 1970s, and he tried to find links. It was a break from recent tradition, where, for two decades, it seemed that excluding those haunting recollections of past successes might lessen the pressure to succeed.

The links Lucia found were perfect. Those previous Herb Brooks championship teams had some high-profile standouts to provide leadership both by skill and personality, and they were bolstered by a rosterful of hard-working over-achievers who would pay any price, in the corners or in front of the nets at either end. What the study may not have disclosed was that those teams also had a little bit of magic, that elusive chemistry that can't be bought, or even leased. It just happens.

Ultimate success generally depends on whether that magical succession of good luck—the breaks—comes your way at the right time. And there was no way to predict the success of chemistry. But part of the magic was hinted at by the almost eerie coincidence that none of the previous three NCAA title teams had won the WCHA title, and all of them had been No. 2 seed among the four finalists. This 2001-02 team ended up precisely in those same circumstances, beyond the control of any design.

The look back is mandatory to fully appreciate the accomplishment of this 2001-2002 team.

Keith Ballard proved he understood the concept of "going to the net."

New Mariucci Arena, built across the street from old Mariucci (formerly Williams) Arena, has been expanded to 10,000 fans—and its own NCAA games.

Chapter 4

Into the modern era

WHO COULD HAVE GUESSED at the growth of college hockey from the University of Minnesota's early days in the sport? Back in 1921-22, I.D MacDonald started the program and fashioned a 6-3-1 record in the first year of hockey at the institution. In Year 2, Emil Iverson took over as coach and stayed for eight years, then it was Frank Pond's turn, for five more seasons. Larry Armstrong coached the Gophers from 1935 through 1947, which included a perfect 18-0-0 season in 1939-40, although there was no such thing as an NCAA tournament in those days.

A rugged young defenseman named John Mariucci came from Eveleth to make an impact on Minnesota hockey—and football—back in 1937. He was named a hockey All-American in 1940. Then he went off to a Hall of Fame career with the Chicago Blackhawks in the National Hockey League, where his legend remains as one of the genuinely toughest characters ever to pull on skates. Meanwhile, in 1947, Doc Romnes became Minnesota's coach, a position he held for five seasons. He brought in such players as Rube Bjorkman, goaltender Larry Ross, and the legendary John Mayasich and Ken Yackel.

Mariucci—the lovable Maroosh—took over the coaching reins next, for the 1952-53 season. The Gophers responded with two of their most successful seasons in Mariucci's first two terms. Led by the Mayasich-Dick Daugherty-Gene Campbell line, with Yackel on defense and goaltender Mattson, the 1952-53 Gophers went 16-4 to win the league title—then called the Midwest Collegiate Hockey League—and were 23-6 overall. That included a 3-2 victory over Rensselaer Polytechnic Institute (RPI) in the NCAA semifinals at Colorado Springs, followed, unfortunately, by a 7-3 loss to Michigan in the final.

The next year, pretty much the same cast of characters led Minnesota to a 15-3-1 record and the championship of the new Western Intercollegiate

Hockey League. Their 23-6-1 overall slate included another trip to Colorado Springs where the heavily favored Gophers beat Boston College 14-1 in the 1954 NCAA semifinals—then were upset 5-4 in overtime by Ned Harkness' RPI Engineers.

Lou Nanne, who went on from All-American status with the Gophers to the NHL as a player and later general manager of the Minnesota North Stars, prefers to consider fellow-Italian Mariucci as his own, personal godfather. More accurately, he was the Godfather of Minnesota Hockey, if not the Godfather of American Hockey, for his outspoken battles to promote U.S. and Minnesota players. Mariucci wasn't against Canadians coming to U.S. colleges to play hockey, but he was adamantly against bringing in older players, who had completed their junior-hockey playing terms at age 20, and came to U.S. colleges as 21-year-old freshmen, only when they didn't get professional offers.

The vast majority of Mariucci's roster came from Minnesota, including players like Herb Brooks from St. Paul Johnson in the mid-1950s, future Minnesota Governor Wendell Anderson, All-Americans such as Yackel, Daugherty, Dick Burg, Mike Pearson, Craig Falkman, future coach Doug Woog and future NHLer Gary Gambucci, and goaltender Jack McCartan. But Mariucci did recruit a sprinkling of Canadian prospects, such as Nanne and Murray Williamson, plus Lorne Grosso and various others. When asked about it, Mariucci's eyes would sparkle and he'd say, "I always like to get one Canadian, just to show I don't discriminate."

If the modern era in hockey is defined by a boundary of 1960, Mariucci was the man who carried Minnesota into that new era. Maroosh's last fling at an NCAA tournament came in 1960-61, when Jerry Norman and Oscar Mahle were scoring leaders, and the "Buzzsaw Line" of Dave Brooks, Len Lilyholm and Gary Schmalzbauer was cutting through opposing defenses. That Gopher team made it to the NCAA tournament in Denver, where it lost 6-1 to Denver, although the Gophers did come back to beat RPI 4-3 in the third-place game.

Glen Sonmor, a native of Hamilton, Ontario, had lost an eye when he was playing for Cleveland in the American Hockey League. He was battling for position in front of the opposing goal when a teammate's slapshot hit him, and with his playing career ended, he was welcomed to come to Minnesota to assist Mariucci. When athletic director Marsh Ryman decided to remove Mariucci in 1966, he hired Sonmor as the new Minnesota coach. Sonmor, who went on to become an outstanding inspirational coach in professional hockey with the Fighting Saints and North Stars in later years, learned his trade from Mariucci. Even though he was a Canadian, Sonmor always built on Maroosh's zealous attempts to favor American hockey players—Minnesota hockey players—and he carried that trait into pro hockey as well.

Under Sonmor, the Gophers didn't tiptoe into the modern era, but pretty much stampeded. Always driven by his own unquenchable enthusiasm, Sonmor tried everything, conventional or not. He recruited a brilliant goaltender from Toronto, named Murray McLachlan, but freshmen weren't allowed to play in those days. So while McLachlan stymied the Gophers in practice, the team was left sputtering without a truly qualified goaltender at the varsity level. Led by future NHLer Gary Gambucci, the Gophers could score goals, but gave up far more. Sonmor tried four goalies that year, and game as they were, he noted that once any of them gave up a goal it would usually start a flurry.

So he decided to change goalies every time the opponent scored. Interesting theory, but the result was disastrous. The Gophers gave up so many goals it looked like Sonmor was changing goalies on the fly. But after that 9-19-1 debut season in 1966-67, Sonmor exacted sweet revenge the next three seasons, with McLachlan in goal.

In 1969-70, the Gophers startled the vastly more experienced WCHA powerhouses by capturing a league title. Minnesota was 18-8 in league play, and 21-12 overall, and over a dozen times victory was achieved after the Gophers were tied or behind in the third period. Antonovich, a pint-sized fireball who stepped in with an electrifying effect, scored 23 goals and 20 assists for 43 points as a freshman to lead the team scoring. The supporting cast included Dean Blais, Bill Butters, Craig Sarner, Mike Kurtz and Wally Olds.

But the Gophers couldn't carry their success through the playoffs. The WCHA tourney brought the top four teams to the Duluth Arena, and Minnesota beat a strong Minnesota-Duluth outfit 3-2 in the semifinals, but it took three overtimes to get it done. The next night, the Gophers gave it their best shot, but Michigan Tech ended their season in a 6-5 thriller.

The next season, 1970-71, Minnesota struggled early, losing the opening series at Duluth 6-3 and 7-2, splitting with Michigan State, then losing 6-5 and 8-5 at Colorado College. In the midst of that 1-5 league start, however, Sonmor made a bold prediction to me. "We're not going to have the kind of team that will contend for the WCHA championship this year," Sonmor said. "But I think by the end of the season, we might have the perfect team to make a run at the NCAA."

More than anyone, he was aware that All-America goaltender Murray McLachlan had graduated, and nobody could replace the brilliant netminder. But Antonovich, Blais, Butters, Sarner, Frank Sanders and brothers Ron and Doug Peltier, John Matschke, and a cast of over-achievers, remained. Incredibly, that Gopher team came back, and after a stirring charge, they made their bid. Losing 4-1 and 3-2 in overtime at Wisconsin—a rivalry at the time that was undoubtedly the most intensely bitter in the country—hardly seemed like a good launch pad to success, but while those losses assured that the Gophers couldn't reach the .500 mark, they came back to Williams Arena and beat Michigan 7-3 and 6-5 in overtime, to finish fifth in the WCHA with their mediocre 9-12-1 record. That sent them back to Madison for the WCHA tournament, full of resolve and motivation. There, the Gophers shocked Wisconsin 4-3, and whipped North Dakota 5-2.

Sonmor's irrepressible drive seemed to force his premonition to come true, and the Gophers were bound for the NCAA tournament at Syracuse, N.Y.—the season ended on March 19-20, in those days. In the semifinals, the Gophers fell behind but made another miracle comeback, and with Antonovich igniting the fuse, the Gophers tied Harvard in the final minute of the third period and beat the Crimson 6-5 in overtime. The next night, however, the rally never came and the Gophers fell 4-2 to an excellent Boston University outfit in the final.

Sonmor, always noting little contributing factors to success or failure, surmised that goaltender Dennis Erickson, an enigmatic junior who alternated with rookie Brad Shelstad all year, had given up three of the four goals low to one side. While walking through the air terminal the next morning, Sonmor noted that Erickson was limping quite noticeably up ahead. Sonmor scoffed. He'd been through the wars, and he was certain that Erickson was trying to shrug off the blame for the championship-game loss by over-playing an imaginary injury.

When the team returned home, Erickson had his knee checked, and it was discovered he had played the championship game with a fractured kneecap. To Sonmor's everlasting credit, he was first to heckle himself for his suspicion.

There was another significant factor to that title game run for a team that rose to an unremarkable 14-17-2 overall season record. A young former Gopher player named Herb Brooks was Sonmor's assistant coach. He had worked hard, and Sonmor, from Day One, said he knew that Brooks would become a fantastic coach some day. But when the Gophers made it to Syracuse, athletic director Marsh Ryman pulled the budgetary strings and refused to allow Brooks to make the trip. Brooks quit, virtually on the spot.

So in 1971, Brooks took on the job as coach of the Minnesota Junior Stars, the team that was the forerunner to the St. Paul Vulcans. He threw together a team that was tough enough to play some outrageously tough outfits in Thunder Bay, and compete well with all comers. Meanwhile, Sonmor, Antonovich and the Gophers went back to the WCHA, but Antonovich was injured early, and things turned sour. Minnesota played its first eight league games on the road, at UMD, Michigan State, Colorado College and Michigan Tech. When that stretch was over, the Gophers stood 1-7. Suddenly, Sonmor was gone, jumping at the opportunity to start up the Minnesota Fighting Saints, St. Paul's entry in the new World Hockey Association. He took Antonovich with him.

New Athletic Director Paul Giel turned to his former football teammate and only trusted hockey source, Ken Yackel. Although Yackel balked, and tried to coax Giel into hiring Brooks, Giel instead coaxed Yackel, a former Big Ten football star as well as All-America hockey defenseman, into taking the job for the remainder of the '71-72 season on an interim basis. Yackel, a student of the game and one of the originators of what would become an enormous summer hockey school concept, stepped in and tried to change over the entire Gopher team to his favored systems in one week. The result? Minnesota was drubbed 15-3 by UMD, right in Williams Arena. To Yackel's credit, he walked in and told the players to forget everything he had told them, and to go back to what they had been doing. Amazingly, the Gophers bounced back to beat UMD 5-3 the next night.

The season ended miserably, with a 7-21 record for a 10th-place WCHA finish and an 8-24 overall mark. But Yackel got through to Giel, and Herb Brooks was hired to take the reins of the faltering program in 1972.

Gophers Jordan Leopold (3), Johnny Pohl (9), and Paul Martin (10) engulfed goaltender Adam Hauser (above) after he had held on to beat Michigan 3-2 in the NCAA semifinals. It took some big saves (below) and support from Leopold and Pohl to subdue the Wolverines and put the Gophers in position to win their first NCAA title after 23 years.

Chapter 5

Those title years

DON LUCIA BACKGROUNDED HIMSELF by going back to study the Herb Brooks coaching era, searching for tidbits that might help inspire the 2001-02 team. He found plenty of them. The three championship teams were just part of the picture of the success that Brooks had ramrodded through, the culmination of the creative Brooks mind.

First of all, as a player, Brooks came out of St. Paul Johnson and skated for John Mariucci at Minnesota. Then he went off to play on several National and Olympic teams. His most famous international playing exploit was when he was the last man cut from the 1960 team that would go on to win the gold medal at Squaw Valley, Calif., where he contacted his dad at the time he was cut, and his dad told him to thank the coach, wish his teammates well, and come home. Brooks, to this day, enjoys telling the story and telling how, instead of feeling like a martyr for missing the gold medal experience, that history indicates "they cut the right guy."

That always makes for a good story, but Brooks also learned plenty from playing international hockey. All the players in the U.S. and Canada at that time were exposed to new and comprehensive styles of play when they faced the Soviet Union, Czechoslovakia or Sweden back in those days, but to almost all of them, the circling, regrouping, collective style the top European teams favored was just something different, something alien to the up-and-down lane style of North American hockey. To Brooks, it was a fascinating departure, and while most North Americans came back from such ventures criticizing the Europeans for not engaging in the traditional rough-and-tumble North American style, Brooks came back with his mind pondering how many different ways there were to play the game.

As the years passed, Brooks would ultimately develop and invent his own hybrid system for playing the game, combining elements of the collective puck-movement style of the Europeans with the hard-nosed North American style he grew up with. That, plus his constantly calculating method for psychological gamesmanship with his players to find key inspirational methods, elevated Brooks to a pedestal far above normal coaches, on either side of the Atlantic.

But in those early years of Brooks's coaching, it was fascinating to watch him develop the things he believed in, modulated by new schemes he'd invent along the way. His own stubborn determination always was present, too, and it seemed to get in the way when he left the University as Sonmor's assistant and took the Minnesota Junior Stars job—forerunner to the St. Paul Vulcans. Instead, that became a quick-study learning experience that altered his perspective.

Brooks put together that fledgling junior team—his first team—intending to have it play a classy, creative style, and it seemed impressive, for awhile. Then the team played in Thunder Bay, which at the time had a collection of some of the toughest, nastiest young players on the face of the earth. The Minnesotans were pretty much mugged. Brooks learned quickly that no matter how skilled his team might be, no matter how idealistic, it would be useless if it wasn't tough enough to ward off the assaults that were out there waiting. On the other hand, being tough enough to handle the worst meant creating sufficient room for the skilled players to flourish.

He made the adjustment with his junior team, and the concept carried over readily to the Gophers, when he stepped behind the bench to take over for the departed Sonmor in 1972. He had Bill Butters and Jimmy Gambucci as co-captains, and he put brash, fiery young Mike Polich and smooth veteran Dean Blais in charge of the offense. Butters paired with Les Auge, who later became an All-America, and the Gophers responded with a rise to a sixth-place finish. Their 12-13-3 WCHA record, and 15-16-3 overall, was a huge improvement over the previous year's 7-21 and 8-24 marks, but it was only the beginning, setting the stage for an incredible run in the following six years of Brooks-led supremacy.

1973-74

In 1973-74, Brooks was coach of the year and the Gophers finished 14-9-5 in the WCHA. That was only good for second, behind a superb 20-6-2 Michigan Tech team. Tech, under the uncompromising leadership of the legendary John MacInnes, had established some control over the Gophers when the two teams finished the regular season in a series at Houghton. Tech skated to 5-2 and 4-1 victories to take the title by an inflated nine points. The

Gophers, however, found some magic in the playoffs. First they beat Michigan 5-1 and 5-4, with the first game making the second total-goal battle somewhat anticlimactic. Next, the Gophers battled Denver to a 3-3 tie, then won 2-1 in the second game to squeeze into the NCAA final four.

The Gophers were thrilled to be heading for Boston Garden, home of the dominating NHL Bruins of Bobby Orr and Phil Esposito. The Gophers had a wide-eyed, home-grown roster led by players such as All-America center Polich, goalies Brad Shelstad and Bill Moen, and a defense that included All-American Auge, future NHLer Joe Micheletti, plus John Perpich, Dick Spannbauer, Doug Falls and Brad Morrow. Up front, Tom Vannelli, Pat Phippen and Warren Miller led a hard-nosed but skilled group that also had John Sheridan, future Olympic star Buzzy Schneider, Cal Cossalter, John Matschke, Tom Dahlheim, and three sets of brothers—future golf star John Harris and his brother Robby, as well as Pat and Mike Phippen, and Bruce and Tim Carlson.

Polich led the team in scoring with 19-33—52, with John Harris next at 17-27—44. But the team-oriented attack also found Schneider and Sheridan contributing 24 goals each. Matschke, one of the holdover heroes from the 1971 NCAA runner-up, had a solid senior year at 15-23—38. Shelstad, the hometown hero who had led Minneapolis Southwest to an incredible 1-0 overtime state championship victory over a powerful Edina team four years earlier, was the star in goal as the Gophers carried their gear into Boston Garden.

Facing the powerful Boston University Terriers in the semifinals, the Gophers were unawed and took command of the game early. But the Terriers came storming back to catch up 4-4 with a couple of late goals. In the closing minutes, it seemed that the rink was tilted from BU's relentless pressure, and it appeared certain the Terriers had enough momentum to blow right past the Gophers. On top of that, BU got a power play. If there was any chance the Gophers would wilt under the pressure, that seemed like the moment it would happen. However, in the face of what looked like imminent collapse, Polich made his move. Killing the penalty, the alert centerman stepped up at center ice to intercept a pass, then he broke in on the left side, 2-on-1. Polich made no mistake, rifling a booming slapshot for a 40-foot shorthanded goal that claimed a 5-4 victory. It may have been the single most important goal in Minnesota history, providing what also might be the single most important victory in Minnesota hockey history. But at the time it was a game of such magnitude that it also could have set up the Gophers for a letdown in the final. No letdown was possible, however, when the championship game opponent was none other than Michigan Tech, the regular-season WCHA champ.

Tech may have assumed it had the clear upper hand, but this was a different Gopher team, surging to a peak it had displayed only in flashes during the regular season. Shelstad was solid in goal, and the game stayed scoreless until Sheridan's goal staked Minnesota to a 1-0 lead late in the first period, with Miller and Phippen assisting. John Perpich scored early in the second for a 2-0 lead, with Morrow and Polich assisting, but Tech countered with a goal by George Lyle. The Gophers took charge in the third, outshooting the Huskies 14-3, for a 39-24 edge in the game, and gained a 3-1 lead when Rob Harris scored at 4:45 on Matschke's assist. The Gophers were so sharp they were never shorthanded in the game. While they failed to score on any of their five power plays, all four Minnesota penalties came in the second period but with coincidental with Tech penalties in every case. Phippen made it 4-1 with Sheridan assisting with 2:43 remaining. Mike Zuke got a goal with 48 seconds left for Tech, although Shelstad's goaltending allowed nothing more. The Gophers had conquered Michigan Tech 4-2 for the first NCAA title in Minnesota's history, finishing with a 22-11-6 overall record.

1975-76

Following up the '74 national title, the Gophers won the WCHA championship in 1975, but lost 6-1 to Michigan Tech in the NCAA championship game in St. Louis. But in 1975-76, the Gophers finished third at 18-13-1 behind Michigan Tech and Michigan State in a fantastic WCHA race, then raced through a dramatic post-season slate. First, the Gophers eliminated Michigan State in a classic league playoff battle at East Lansing. After a 2-2 tie in the first of a total-goal series, the Gophers got a huge goal from Pat Phippen and beat the Spartans 7-6 in triple overtime to gain the NCAA.

At the NCAA final four at Denver, Minnesota beat Boston University in a game that featured a controversial bench-clearing brawl in the semifinals. An incident near the Minnesota bench ignited into a wild fracas that saw each team lose a player. Minnesota lost future NHL star defenseman Russ Anderson. But after showing they were ready to play it any way necessary, the Gophers held their cool and dispatched the Terriers 4-2.

Minnesota beat—you guessed it—Michigan Tech in the NCAA final in a 6-4 gem, upending the WCHA season champion Huskies for the second time in three straight NCAA title games. This time, however, Minnesota needed a sensational comeback over the second and third periods to capture the big prize. The Gophers trailed 3-0 in the first 12 minutes before Tom Vannelli scored a goal. Goaltender Jeff Tscherne had a rocky start, and was replaced by Mohr after that three-goal Tech barrage.

Linemates Vannelli, Phippen and Miller, and defensemen Joe Micheletti and Morrow, all were returnees from that first NCAA title, and the runner-up finish. Brooks had supplemented them with forwards Tom Younghans and Tom Gorence, both of whom went on to play in the NHL; future Olympian Phil Verchota, Bob Fish, Tim Rainey, Bryan Fredrickson, Ken Yackel Jr., and hard-nosed hustlers Mark Lambert, Dan Bonk and Bruce Lind. Big Tony Dorn from Thief River Falls was another element. On defense, Micheletti and Morrow found adequate help from future NHL and Hall of Famer Reed Larson, future Olympian Bill Baker, plus Jim Boo, Joe Baker and Robin Larson. Goaltenders were Tscherne, Mohr and a rookie named Steve Janaszak.

But the fuse that ignited the Gophers was Vannelli, an always-pleasant little center nicknamed "Choirboy" by Brooks for his smiling, soft-spoken demeanor. But the Choirboy was a tenacious competitor, a fact that was evident by watching him take faceoffs. Or, by compiling points at key moments of big games. Vannelli's goal with 2:55 left in the first period came on a power play set-up by future North Star Younghans and Phippen. Joe Micheletti, with assists from Reed Larson and Vannelli, cut it to 3-2 at 2:55 of the second, also on a power play. Bill Baker made it 3-3 with the third straight goal for the Gopher power play, as Vannelli and Phippen assisted at 10:26. Two minutes later, Gorence converted a set-up by Reed Larson, and Minnesota's fourth straight goal had forged a 4-3 lead on the strength of a 16-3 Minnesota shot advantage in the second period.

Tech rebounded to gain a 4-4 tie when Nels Goddard scored with 36 seconds left in the middle period—the only goal Mohr yielded in the second and third periods—but the Gophers didn't flinch. Phippen's goal, with Vannelli and Reed Larson assisting, broke the deadlock at 8:37 of the final period. And Miller, with assists from four-year cronies Vannelli and Phippen, closed out the 6-4 triumph with a goal with 30 seconds remaining. That meant Vannelli had followed up his opening goal with four assists, including Phippen's game-winner and Miller's last-minute clincher.

By scoring 1-4—5 in the championship game, Vannelli wound up leading the title team in scoring (26-43—69), while Miller (26-31—57) and Phippen (17-33—50) made that line 1-2-3 in team scoring. Younghans added 19-24—43 and Reed Larson added 13-29—42 from the right point, as Minnesota wound up 28-14-2 overall, and on a roll that wouldn't stop.

1978-79

How good was the 1978-79 Gopher team? Not only was it good enough to win the national championship, but Brooks went off to coach the U.S. Olympic team the next year, and he was totally justified in selecting goaltender Janaszak, defensemen Bill Baker and Mike Ramsey, and forwards Neal Broten, Steve Christoff, Rob McClanahan, Eric Strobel and Phil Verchota—eight players from that championship team—to form the core of the 1980 Olympic team. Goaltender Jim Jetland joined Janaszak, while the defense consisted of Bill Baker, Ramsey, Bob Bergloff, Peter Hayek, Joe Baker, Mike Greeder, Brian Zins, Bart Larson, Steve Pepper and Jay Larson. Up front, Neal Broten, Christoff, McClanahan, Strobel and Verchota were joined by sniper Tim Harrer, Don Micheletti, Steve Ulseth, Kevin Hartzell, Dave Terwilliger, Jeff Teal, Brad Doshan, John Meredith and Wayne Larson.

After winning the title in 1976, the Gophers dipped to seventh in 1976-77, then rose back to fourth in '77-78, and to second in 1978-79, a season that might go down as the WCHA's best ever, from the standpoint of overall talent. Aside from the Gophers, Minnesota-Duluth had players like Olympians Mark Pavelich and John Harrington, and Curt Giles, who was soon to become the best defenseman in North Stars history. Wisconsin had center Mark Johnson and defenseman Bob Suter—two more Olympians. North Dakota had Olympian David Christian and a herd of future pros, such as defensemen Howard Walker and Marc Chorney, and forwards Mark Taylor and Kevin Maxwell. With all those standouts, the league scoring champion was Dave Delich of Colorado College.

But as magnificent as those Gophers were, they couldn't quite pull off the magic double of the WCHA and NCAA titles. The WCHA race went down to the final regular-season series when North Dakota came to then-Williams Arena. Minnesota won the first game 5-2, climbing to within one point of the first-place Sioux. But North Dakota won the finale 4-2 on David Christian's hat trick, to claim the league title with a 22-10 record to the Gophers 20-11-1 mark. But, sure enough, Brooks got the Gophers back together in the WCHA tournament, beating a very good Minnesota-Duluth outfit 2-1 and 6-3 while North Dakota dispatched Wisconsin, sending both teams to the NCAA tournament. The Gophers had to conquer Bowling Green to advance to the final four at Detroit's old Olympia, and they did that, 6-3. In Detroit, Minnesota overcame New Hampshire 4-3 in the semifinals, to gain a title-game showdown against North Dakota.

The Gophers jumped ahead when Christoff scored 4:11 into the first period on Verchota's feed. Meredith made it 2-0 at 8:05, with Strobel and Ulseth assisting. The Fighting Sioux fought back for a goal that read Bill Himmelright from Mark Taylor and Kevin Maxwell—all three future pros. But Billy Baker made it 3-1 at 19:22 of the first, with Don Micheletti and Neal Broten assisting. Maxwell cut it to 3-2 with the only goal of the second period, on assists from Cary Eades and Taylor at 18:02. But at 2:48 of the third period, Broten chased after a puck sliding into the Sioux zone as North Dakota goaltender Bob Iwabuchi came out after it. Broten won the race, but barely, lunging to chip the puck up and over Iwabuchi and into the goal as Broten sprawled on the ice. That goal, at 2:48, is another of the most memorable tallies in Gopher history and it stood up through that epic final, as Janaszak held off everything except a goal by Chorney at 9:56, coming from Charlie Burggraf and Taylor, who notched his third assist of the game.

Minnesota outshot the Fighting Sioux 35-28 in the title game, and completed an amazing stretch of three national championships in six years. Herb Brooks drifted off into the Gopher history books, having accomplished amazing things—things that only could be outdone by what he was about to do with the Miracle-on-Ice Team USA at Lake Placid one year later.

Dan Welch (23), who regained his eligibility at midseason, and Pat O'Leary looked for a rebound in a tough series at Duluth.

The deadly shot of Jeff Taffe was worth 34 goals, and some spectacular saves, such as this one by UMD goalie Adam Coole.

Grant Potulny (18) and Jeff Taffe went to the net to score key goals for the Gophers.

Chapter 6

Coming up short

IF YOU COULD FLASH FORWARD from the date of that third Gopher NCAA title—March 24, 1979—and checked the driver's licenses of the 2001-02 championship team, you would find that junior forward Nick Anthony, who was born on January 30, 1979, was the only member of this championship team who had been born at the time of the last previous Gopher championship. And he was a mere 2 months old.

All three of those 1970s championship teams were savored by zealous Gopher fans, who might have stashed them away to make room for the certainty of more to come. But just as all three of those teams had magic going for them, since then, the Gophers became known as a team that could almost always get to the NCAA tournament, but continually fell short of the ultimate objective. With each passing year, it seemed as if succeeding coaches and officials tended to refrain from mentioning those title teams, as if distancing themselves would give each new team a fresh chance.

Don Lucia changed all that, and before his third season, he went back and totally embraced what went into those championship years, using that research to help weave the fabric for the 2001-02 championship run.

When Brooks left the University after the 1979 championship, it was for a year's leave of absence to assemble and coach the 1980 U.S. Olympic team for its odyssey to Lake Placid. When the U.S. beat the Soviet Union in the classic penultimate game of the Olympics, Brooks sat in the small office at Lake Placid, where he was avoiding the media and its usual post-game interrogation. He looked across the desk at me and smiled. Then he said: "This is going to cost Giel a ton."

Classic Brooks. He fully intended to return to the University of Minnesota, and he knew his success at Lake Placid would translate to a huge raise from athletic director Paul Giel. As things worked out, Brooks got other offers, and actually went to Davos, Switzerland, to coach professionally for a year when no National Hockey League offer was affirmed. Back at Minnesota, Giel, who had elevated assistant coach Brad Buetow to interim coach while Brooks was gone, installed Buetow as official head coach.

Buetow's team had done surprisingly well with all the Olympic departures gone. Tim Harrer, Don Micheletti and freshman Aaron Broten led the way. One year later, Neal Broten returned to join his brother, Aaron, and the 1981 team came infinitely close to another NCAA title. That would have elevated Buetow, and the Gopher program, to historic proportions, but the team came apart in the title game.

The 1981 team was the clearcut favorite to win it all, with the Roseau line of Neal and Aaron Broten and Butsy Erickson reunited for part of the season, and joined by Steve Ulseth, Kevin Hartzell and Mike Knoke to lead the way. After winning the league title and advancing to the final four, Minnesota played as close to a perfect game as possible in whipping Michigan Tech 7-2 in the semifinals, in a splendid display of every facet of the game in the Duluth Arena, as it was known then. But then the Gophers were ambushed by an aroused Wisconsin team in a 6-3 title-game shocker. The Badgers defused the Gopher power play effectively to take leads of 3-0 after one and 4-0 in the second before Minnesota started to play with the required focus or intensity.

When it was over, Wisconsin coach Badger Bob Johnson led a celebration out into the night that was handled with great delicacy by the Duluth police department. The cops saw the horde of red-clad Badger fans, realized they were overmatched, and ultimately closed off Superior Street to allow the party to go long into the night. At one point, Coach Johnson was spotted standing atop a parked car, leading cheers for the crazed fans. Meanwhile, the Gophers were not about to shed their disappointment easily. In a tear-filled DECC dressing room, Gopher defenseman Brian Zins broke the silence with a wisecrack. "Every once in a while, Avis rents more cars than Hertz," said Zins. "But they're still No. 2."

Buetow had some outstanding teams, and some strong players, such as current assistant coach Mike Guentzel, Gary Shopek, Tony Kellin and Dave Jensen on defense, forwards like Pat Micheletti, Wally Chapman, Tom Rothstein, Steve Griffith, Scott Bjugstad, Tim Bergland and Rick Erdall up front, and goaltenders such as Paul Ostby, Frank Pietrangelo and John Blue.

In 1983, Minnesota again was No. 1 in the league, and reached the final four at Grand Forks, but lost 5-3 to Harvard in the semifinals, clearing the way for Wisconsin to claim the crown. The Gophers played a quarterfinal

NCAA total-goal series at Boston College at the end of the 1984-85 season, and they beat the Eagles 7-5 the first night. But BC stormed back to win 4-1 in the second game, snatching the two-game series 9-8. That meltdown turned out to be Buetow's last game as Gopher coach.

Doug Woog's tenure brought many more close calls. In Woog's first nine seasons, the Gophers won three WCHA titles and finished second the other six years. In Woog's first year in the league (1985-86), the Gophers swept two games at Boston University in the NCAA quarterfinals, but fell 6-4 to Michigan State in the semifinals at Providence. The next year, a quarterfinal total-goal victory at Boston College sent the Gophers to Detroit, where Michigan State again ended the Gophers run with a 5-3 semifinal victory.

Minnesota won the WCHA title by an 11-point bulge in 1987-88, and got revenge against Michigan State by sweeping 4-2, 4-3 victories from the Spartans in the NCAA quarterfinals. Again the Gophers looked like the NCAA favorite, with Hobey Baker Award goaltender Robb Stauber in the nets, but at Lake Placid, the Gophers fell 3-2 to St. Lawrence in the semifinals. Maine also lost in the semis, creating the last third-place game in NCAA tournament annals. As usual, the frustration and disappointment of playing in the final night's "preliminary" led to some ragged and rugged play, and at one point, the officials were gathered at the scoring table to sort out penalties, and Stauber reached over for the puck, which was left idle nearby, and slid it 180 feet toward the Maine goal. Naturally, Black Bear goaltender Garth Snow made the stop, then he sent it back, toward the Gopher goal. The two continued to flip 180-foot shots at each other, and the crowd loved it, but the officials skated out angrily and confiscated the puck.

As the officials returned to the scorer's table, Stauber went to the Minnesota bench, apparently for a drink of water. He also slipped a spare puck into his glove, returned to the nets, and when nobody was watching, he dropped the puck on the ice and resumed his game with Snow. The crowd roared at what was clearly the high point of a 5-2 Maine victory, but the officials again reacted as if the decorum and sanctity of the sport had been threatened, taking the puck and admonishing the goalies. Lake Superior State went on to beat St. Lawrence in the final, 4-3 in overtime, and the NCAA never again held a third-place game. Presumably that was because of the disorderly play, and not because the goaltenders violated acceptable deportment.

Woog's team again made it to the final four the following season, in 1988-89. Led by Stauber, Tom Chorske, Dave Snuggerud and Todd Richards, the Gophers won the WCHA title by 14 points with a superb 27-6-2 record.

Their overall record wound up 34-11-3, and Stauber had even better statistics than in his Hobey season. But Minnesota fans were left gasping for one more victory at the end. The Gophers beat Wisconsin in a pair of 4-2 games in the NCAA quarterfinals to reach the final four, which was right down University Av., in the Saint Paul Civic Center. Minnesota beat Maine 7-4 in the semifinals, but Harvard beat the Gophers 4-3 in sudden-death overtime in the final, a game that observers still claim might have been the greatest ever played. A highlight of that game was when new Hobey Baker winner Lane MacDonald scored a goal on Stauber, the previous year's Hobey winner.

But that was about it. Only twice in the 12 years after 1989 did the Gophers even reach the final four, which became the "Frozen Four" a few years later, when the NCAA deemed its basketball tournament the only event worthy of its "copyrighted" Final Four designation. The 1994 team reached the elite NCAA field in the Civic Center, but Boston University thumped the Gophers 4-1 in the semifinals. In 1995, Minnesota made it to Providence but fell 7-3 to BU.

A seemingly endless list of skilled players under Woog also included forwards Jay Cates, Paul Broten, Dave Snuggerud, Cory Laylin, brothers Peter, Ben and Casey Hankinson, Ken Gernander, Trent Klatt, Justin McHugh, Grant Bischoff, Corey Millen, Craig Johnson, Jeff Nielsen, Joe Dziedzic, All-American Brian Bonin, Ryan Kraft, defensemen Lance Pitlick, Dave Espe, Luke Johnson, brothers Todd and Travis Richards, Larry Olimb, Doug Zmolek, Chris McAlpine and Mike Crowley, and goaltenders Stauber, Jeff Stolp, Tom Newman, Jeff Callinan, Jeff Moen and Steve DeBus.

But despite all the impressive names, and all the painstaking work to achieve 13 consecutive appearances at least in the NCAA tournament quarterfinals or regionals, the Gophers started to misfire. And when fortunes sagged, a lot of exceptional players had to turn in their equipment for the summer before the tournaments were held in 1998, 1999 and 2000.

Chapter 7

Lucia always a winner

As Don Lucia learned, nothing would be automatic about reinstating the glory years at Minnesota. The former Colorado College coach knew all he needed to know about the Minnesota program, growing up and playing high school hockey in Grand Rapids. He played defense in the glory days at Grand Rapids, before the Indians changed their name to the more politically-correct Thunderhawks, and he played on four state tournament teams there, including the championship teams of 1975 and 1976. The Indians took home the third-place trophy in 1974, Lucia's freshman year, and 1977, when he was a senior.

Lucia went on to play defense at Notre Dame, and even though he was drafted by the Philadelphia Flyers, he chose to go into coaching, starting as an assistant at Alaska-Fairbanks from 1981-85, before he moved to Alaska-Anchorage from 1985-87. He then went back to Alaska-Fairbanks as head coach from 1987-93, and led the Nanooks to four winning seasons in six years with an overall 113-87-10 record.

In the fall of 1993, Lucia was hired to replace former Gopher coach Brad Buetow at Colorado College. Buetow had assembled a team that had risen to a .500 season and was predicted to contend and maybe even win the 1992-93 league title. Instead, the Tigers came apart at the seams, plunging to last place at 8-20 (6-26 in the WCHA), and Buetow was dismissed. It was far more than just a metaphorical coming-in-from-the-cold when Lucia moved down from Alaska to the Pike's Peak foothills. The Colorado College Tigers had not had a winning season in 13 consecutive years following their 1992-93 nosedive. So as Lucia took over, the WCHA coaches predicted the Tigers would be last again in 1993-94.

Instead, and incredibly, Lucia's first-year Tigers rose to a 23-11-5 record and CC's first WCHA championship in 37 years. As if that wasn't impressive enough, Lucia guided the Tigers to another WCHA title in 1994-95, and made it an unprecedented three straight WCHA titles when they won in 1995-96, winning a school-record 33 games. Never in league history had any team won three straight titles, and Lucia followed up his three straight league championships by bringing the Tigers in fourth, third and second, keeping them in contention, and compiling an overall record of 166-68-18 in six years at Colorado College.

While CC was recording three firsts, a second, a third and a fourth, the Gophers were going the other direction, dropping from a 20-year run of over-.500 contention to sixth place in 1997-98 and fifth in 1998-99. Coach Doug Woog had encountered some problems in the last four years of his 14-year reign, but only after an extremely successful first 10 years. Woog's tenure was highlighted by his insistence that the Gophers would take John Mariucci's dream to an extreme by recruiting only Minnesota players to skate for the Gophers. But as things unraveled, Woog belittled players frequently, leading to some complaints. Then he was accused of some NCAA violations.

Athletic director Mark Dienhart defended and excused Woog after several allegations of NCAA infractions—some of which were verified. But his patience seemed to run out about the time the team's on-ice success started to fade. Dienhart decided to make the move after the 1998-99 season and hired the squeaky-clean Lucia to leave Colorado College and come back to his home state to take the helm of the University of Minnesota.

The move was heralded by some, but it ruffled some traditionalists' feathers, because they had grown accustomed to the natural progression of "M"-men as Gopher coach—from Mariucci to Sonmor to Brooks to Buetow to Woog, over half a decade. Lucia was a home-stater, but he had played his college hockey at Notre Dame. Lucia's soft-spoken charm, handsome good looks—including his long, dark wavy hair—plus the success of his CC teams, conquered the skeptics. It wasn't easy. Nor was it immediate, compared to his first-year title at Colorado College.

When Lucia was introduced at Mariucci Arena, there were about 100 media types and school officials gathered, and Lucia was overwhelmed by the sheer number of those in attendance. He turned to his wife, Joyce, and said, "Can you believe this?" He was used to much less attention from the tidy group that might have showed at Colorado Springs, in the smaller media-market coverage area of Colorado College.

Lucia expressed the same feeling to me after that media session, and I cautioned him, and Joyce, that they shouldn't anticipate such a media throng. They might be there at the first day of practice, too, I suggested, but on Day

2 of practice, he might wonder where everybody went, because the Twin Cities media would be off covering the Vikings, or Gopher football, or the NBA's Timberwolves (to say nothing of the NHL Wild, when they started play a year later).

In retrospect, after the Gophers won the 2002 title, Lucia recalled that day of his press conference.

"You were right," Lucia said. "There was an initial crush. One thing we found, we got more media attention the second half of season, after the Vikings were over. The Vikings get the crush of the media attention. We get our share, but it's really after the Vikings season ends that we see more TV cameras coming around.

"I think the first year is overwhelming, in any job. I've always said you're happy when the first year is over, because it's a transition, trying to get your family settled, getting four kids into new schools, and we didn't get into our new house until August. I was worried about the kids and my wife, being ripped apart from her friends and her identity, and in new surroundings. Then it took some time trying to get to know all the players. When you're at a job for a while, you get into a comfort zone of walking in and going to work and feeling comfortable. But you don't even get comfortable at work for a year."

Freshman Barry Tallackson dashed through a pack of Bulldogs for a poke-check goal.

Matt Koalska was foiled on this wraparound bid, and scored only nine goals all season, but he was saving No. 10 for the NCAA final, where he scored it for the last-minute tying goal that forced overtime.

Troy Riddle (21) was in perfect position, but Maine goaltender Matt Yeats didn't leave a rebound.

Chapter 8

Growing up with expectations

THE GOPHER PLAYERS ALL TALKED ABOUT HOW, growing up, they became accustomed to Minnesota making it to the NCAA tournament, year after year. By the time they were playing in high school or junior hockey, the Gophers started ending their seasons a bit early, and missed the playoffs. In 1997-98, the Gophers failed to reach the selected 12 for the NCAA. In 1998-99, they missed it again. When Lucia was named to replace Doug Woog as coach, the Gophers also failed to make the NCAA for the 1989-2000 season.

Jordan Leopold, the All-American and Hobey Baker-winning defenseman, wasn't altogether typical of the prototype Gopher, because he left high school to play at the new USA Hockey development camp in Ann Arbor, Mich. However, he still had the typical view of the Minnesota program, and followed it closely, even from afar.

"Definitely, growing up in Minnesota, you think about Gopher hockey, because it's one of the most important programs in the country," Leopold said. "There are other great programs, like Michigan. But at Michigan—it's not even close, because their football program is so good. Here we're fortunate that we're in a situation where our hockey program can be the top program.

"While I was at Ann Arbor, I always got filled in on what was going on with the Gophers. It used to be kind of automatic that they'd be up at the top, going to the national tournament every year. But the year I was at Ann Arbor, I guess it was pretty bad. They were below .500, and got beat by Duluth in the playoffs. It was not the usual Gopher hockey season."

Nick Angell, another senior defenseman on the championship team, took a decidedly different route to that pinnacle. He stayed in high school at Duluth East, where the Greyhounds were a perennial state tournament threat. He looked closely at Minnesota-Duluth and Minnesota, and on one recruiting trip, he could have wiped the Gophers from consideration, but he saw beyond what seemed the ultimate insult.

Angell and his dad had been recruited, but only by Minnesota assistant coaches, and when it was time for their campus visit, they met coach Woog in his office. They talked for a while, but after Woog made a couple of hesitant comments, it became obvious to them that the coach didn't know which prospect he was talking to. When confronted, Woog had to admit he didn't know who Nick was. Still, Angell, who had indicated he was leaning toward UMD, grew to like Woog on some intense follow-up visits, and chose Minnesota in spite of the slight.

"When I was looking at colleges, I wanted to go to UMD, but I looked at all the NCAA appearances Minnesota had made," Angell said. "They'd go to all of them. They missed the NCAA my senior year in high school, but that was like the only year they missed that I knew of. You've got to like a team's chances to win it all when they go to all the tournaments, and that made sense to me, especially, coming from East, where we had lost two games in the two years I played high school.

"We lost in the championship game to Edina my junior year, and that was our only loss that whole season. Then my senior year, we lost one game, 7-5 to Grand Rapids, and won the state title. So I had only played in two lost games in two years in high school.

"Then when I came here, we might have assumed we'd make it to the NCAA, but we had a pretty bad year."

After 13 consecutive appearances in the NCAA tournament, missing the tournament in 1997-98 might have seemed startling to Gopher boosters. When the new freshmen came in and the Gophers missed the NCAA tournament again in 1998-99, it was grounds for a coaching change. And when Lucia's first team missed the tournament in 1999-2000, it meant the Gophers suddenly had missed it for three straight years.

The players wearing the giant "M" on their chests, who grew up certain that the Gophers would reach the post-season event every year, were now caught up in the new, and distasteful, routine of NOT making the tournament. And this new crop of players found themselves personally part of the new routine, and helpless to do anything about it.

The tight ship that Woog had run for several years seemed to be listing badly, and the seas seemed to be getting increasingly rough. The administration suddenly found itself having to defend Woog against allegations of NCAA violations. As Mark Dienhart and his administration battled to defend his honor, then their honor, a large-scale basketball scandal over academic fraud erupted and dwarfed the hockey program's problems. The hockey hassles must have seemed like a persistent little nuisance grassfire compared to the basketball mansion being in flames. When the hockey team's success started to drop as well, however, the decision was made. Woog was dismissed, although it was cloaked as his decision, and he was kept on at the same salary to sell suites that were being planned a couple years ahead for Mariucci Arena.

A lot of alumni, who had been muttering about the program's deterioration, celebrated the move when Lucia was brought in. The faltering record was the last straw, although some still thought an "M" Man should have gotten the job. The players, most of them at least, seemed to think the time had come for a change. But not all of them celebrated. Nick Angell was apprehensive.

"I liked coach Woog," Angell said. "You could always go up to the front of the bus and shoot the shit with him. I still see him and talk over what happened the past weekend. A lot of guys didn't have choice things to say about him, but I said, 'Hey, this is the guy who brought me here.' He never did anything wrong to me. I got to play a lot under him. You've got to remember, all the guys here used to be the best player on their high school team. A lot of guys who didn't get a chance to play much might not have liked him so much, which is the case with anybody, because guys get frustrated.

"I was a little concerned when Don Lucia was named the new coach. I wasn't sure if he'd remember me or not. The one time I got injured in a game was when we were playing at Colorado College my freshman year and Coach Lucia was coaching there. We were losing 7-1 and it was pretty frustrating. Ian Petersen speared me. I lost my temper and I broke my stick across his helmet, and when everybody came running over to break us up, the ref tackled me. He fell on my leg as we went down, and I was out with a sprained ankle.

"So then they named Lucia as the new coach here, I wasn't sure how it would go," Angell added, laughing. "I don't think he had any big problem with me, although it took me two and a half years to get back on the power play."

Nick Anthony closed fast, looking for any rebound that might come loose.

Goaltender Adam Hauser opened his senior year with a "disastrous" first game at North Dakota.

Chapter 9

The transition to 'team'

WHEN LUCIA TOOK OVER, he found a lot things contributing to prevent the Gophers from being in sync. The Gophers were .500—going 13-13-2 for sixth place in the WCHA and 20-19-2 overall in Lucia's first year—and while that wasn't up to "old" traditional Gopher standards, it represented an upturn from the "new" tradition after two straight years under .500 (17-22 and 15-19-9).

At CC, Lucia had been impressed with the Gopher talent, even though his Tigers had established something resembling mastery in their meetings with Minnesota. In Lucia's term at CC, the Tigers had gone 19-7 against Minnesota overall, including CC victories in all nine of the teams' meeting over the last two years Lucia was there.

"I think the big issue I had, coming here, was that the team was very fractured," said Lucia. There was no camaraderie whatsoever; and it seemed like guys were more worried about themselves than about the team. The older guys kind of mistreated the younger guys, which I think becomes divisive. One of the first things I did was to abolish initiations, or hazings. I was adamant. I told the captains they'd lose their letter if it happened, under their watch.

"My objective was to try to get our young guys involved in the program. It's tough enough to be a freshman and try to adjust to new surroundings, going to school, being away from home, trying to fit in with the team, then if you're going to get hazed. I heard the stories, of older guys taking advantage of younger guys. Nate Miller was a great captain that first year in helping to do away with all that stuff."

The players noted the difference immediately. Particularly those players who had been freshmen the year before Lucia came in—the same nucleus of the 2001-02 championship team as seniors.

It started with the hazings. It used to be a routine, possibly even dating back to the days when Woog played for Mariucci. While it wasn't a part of Sonmor's teams, and wasn't a major issue on Buetow's teams, it had grown during the Woog regime. While Woog didn't order it, he more or less looked the other way when the veterans would organize a big annual team party early in training camp. Generally, the upper-classmen would work over the freshmen, at those functions, gang-tackling the rookies and enjoying it most when the freshmen resisted strenuously. The result always was some grotesque chop jobs for haircuts. Sometimes the veterans would shave the rookies' heads, and invariably, the hair being cut was not confined to their heads. It became a matter of survival. While such sessions might have assured that there would be no prima donnas among the rookies, if it had any other positive bonding effect it wasn't evident, and the whole procedure was divisive as well as extremely distasteful and terrifying to the rookies.

"I just go back to my high school days and college days," said Lucia. "I never experienced any hazing anywhere I went. And I wouldn't allow it as a coach. I don't know how something like hazing could help, it could only divide. I've never been part of winning teams that didn't get along great. They cared about each other."

When the 2001-02 seniors were freshmen, the seniors included some very good players, including Wyatt Smith and Reggie Berg. By recollection, the championship seniors remembered those veterans as immensely skilled, but eager to carry out the team tradition of distancing themselves from the freshmen, who were left to struggle to find their way into the team structure.

Defenseman Nick Angell recalled how even moving into the dorm was a revelation as a freshman. Angell, who is 6-feet tall and weighs over 200, was assigned to room with Pat O'Leary, who is 6-2 and 205.

"I was assigned to a room E554 in Comstock Hall," said Angell. "I was rooming with O'Leary, and our room was the smallest room I'd ever been in. But it turned out to be the biggest dorm room any of the freshmen had. Some guys had played a couple years of junior, and most played at least one. I realize I might have been better prepared if I had played a year of junior, because I'd never even washed my own clothes. Or cooked. I had to learn how to make mac-and-cheese! I remember lying on the cot in our room, staring at the ceiling and thinking about how surprising it was to be in such a tiny room at such a big school, thinking about going to the first practice…and scared shitless.

"My freshman year was the last year of 'initiations,' " said Angell. "There was a freshman party, and older guys would shave the freshmen, and not just their heads. That had been going on for quite a while, I guess. I remember thinking even then that 'When I 'm a senior there won't be any of this.' "

Jordan Leopold, who hit the ice as a standout from his first day as a freshman, agreed, but also recalls that he never knew what to expect as a rookie.

"When we came in as freshmen, we had no expectations," Leopold said. "Because they had done so badly, I think the older players just wanted to beat what the other years had been doing. As freshmen, we didn't know what it would be like. Just adjusting to living in the dorms, going to class, to study halls, that was tough enough. And to not have a car, especially when you're in a town that you know so well, that was tough. But you work through it.

"I was treated the same as others...and treated badly...but it wasn't horrible," Leopold added. "There was no team chemistry, or bonding. Right after our freshman year, it changed. When you first come into a situation, you don't know what's going on. You don't want to be all nervous and tense, so you just go along with it. You've got six or eight guys who came in with you, and that's it. But you've got to remember, the guys above us were pretty good players."

Johnny Pohl, coming in fresh from being named "Mr. Hockey" for his record scoring exploits at Red Wing High School, remembers his on-ice struggles more than any hazing problems from his first year.

"For any freshman, the first year of college hockey is a blur," said Pohl. "As a freshman, I just wanted to play and be part of the team."

Pohl recalls games and incidents within games to a degree that causes his teammates to shake their heads in amazement. Whenever any of them couldn't remember exact details of a game, they'd simply say, "You'll have to ask Johnny Pohl."

His role as unofficial team historian will come into greater use later on, but he was not the only one who retained specific incidents with great clarity.

Angell also recalled those freshman practices.

"It was even tough on the ice, at practice," said Angell. "As freshmen, if you stole the puck from some of the seniors, they'd two-hand you. I remember O'Leary scored a goal against a couple of seniors in a scrimmage and somebody shot a slapshot and hit him in the helmet. Just for scoring a goal, he gets a slapshot off his head!

"We'd go on road trips that year and we'd all talk about things. Like, one freshman said he roomed with Wyatt Smith, and Wyatt never said a thing to him the whole weekend. How are you going to play and feel part of the team if your roommate is a senior who hasn't talked to you all weekend?

"I remember we were having a scrimmage once during practice, and Wyatt Smith circled back in his own end with the puck, then started stickhandling up the ice. Woog was screaming at him, 'Move the puck....Move the puck....' but Wyatt kept carrying it. Woog kept screaming at him, as Wyatt went all the way into the offensive zone, then all of a sudden he circled back to center ice, still with the puck, and came by the bench. Woog was still screaming at him to move the puck, and Smith came by the bench and yelled, '(Bleep) you!' to Woog, and kept right on going, carrying the puck back into the offensive zone. I remember as a freshman, standing there on the bench and witnessing the whole thing. I couldn't believe it."

In Woog's first 10 years as coach, there was none of that sort of disarray. One of the reasons might have been that Bill Butters was Woog's top assistant. Butters, a hard-core pro with the Fighting Saints and later the Minnesota North Stars, was considered an unexcelled teacher of young defensemen, at any level. As good as he was on the ice, Butters was at least as effective mingling with the players in the dressing room. Instead of isolating himself in the coaches' dressing room, he obviously enjoyed joking with the players. Butters was always an exceptional judge of people, and if any problem seemed to be developing, he could either head it off or at least apprise Woog of it. So there were no such problems.

The departure of Butters created a large void between the players and the coaching staff, which apparently widened over the next four years until the change in head coaches.

"Johnny Pohl and the other seniors were only sophomores when I came," said Lucia. "None of the rest of the players were here yet, so they wouldn't notice any change from the coaching change. As for changes, I'm not aware what happened before I got here."

The players noticed, though. Angell, perhaps the most appreciative of Woog's guidance, said the difference was immediate.

"When coach Lucia came in, he said no more initiations or hazing," Angell said. "There are still some practical jokes, like the freshmen falling down and then finding that someone had put clear tape on their skate blades. Or we make the freshmen carry the equipment. But everybody gets along. The biggest difference between this year and my freshman year is that everybody on this team is so much closer."

Leopold concurred. "Some hazing still happens," Leopold added, acknowledging that it became more fun by his senior year. "The kind of hazing is not up to a coach; the guys are the ones who make the rules and follow them. You're dealing with grownups, not minors anymore.

"No question, the biggest difference between this year and our freshman year is in how we worked together with the freshmen this year. We made that decision right after our freshman year. Coach Lucia came in and it was a breath of fresh air. Nothing against Doug Woog. Woog's a great guy, and when you thought about Gopher hockey, you thought about him. Who other than Doug Woog?

"But I think everybody, including the players, felt we needed a change, and when you change coaches, you also change perspective."

Grant Potulny and Jeff Taffe fight for a rebound against UMD.

Big Nick Angell, the late-blooming senior defenseman, arrived with force to support goalie Adam Hauser.

Goalie Adam Hauser and defensemen Keith Ballard (13) and Nick Angell (26) defend against Maine.

Chapter 10

Teenagers grow up fast

IF YOU CALCULATE THE AGES of each class on every team, the Gophers off 2001-02 were undoubtedly the youngest team, age-wise, in the WCHA. And maybe in the country. Particularly Division One. It might even stand up as some sort of record, because the championship Minnesota outfit might remain the last "young" championship team for the foreseeable future. The trend developed through the 1990s in college hockey was for Division One college coaches to check their bets; instead of fighting it out over high school kids who would be 18- or 19-year-old college freshmen, they let the kids finish high school and go off to someplace like the United States Hockey League (USHL) and play another year or two. With 65 games a year, obviously, any player will improve by the added experience of more games for more years.

Philosophically, that's not new. It dates back to the John Mariucci era, when Minnesota stood alone against the comparatively elderly recruits going from Tier I Canadian junior programs to Denver, Michigan Tech, Michigan, North Dakota and Colorado College. While Mariucci fought it, the Gopher belief in taking high school grads and developing them was something that Minnesota teams of old used to benefit from. The Gophers would pluck off the best players from the fantastic Minnesota state high school program, and compete against older foes with those teenagers as they grew and matured. Mariucci did it that way, as did Sonmor, Brooks, Buetow and Woog.

But as the years passed without an NCAA title, and the program seemed to be falling behind the older, more diverse and competitive opponents, some outside observers, who lacked the instate-hockey devotion to the Gopher philosophy, questioned the validity of trying to compete with younger prospects. As Woog's teams kept falling short, and Woog continued to stick with only Minnesotans and mostly young ones at that, critics thought they had an easy answer. Clearly, they had slipped from the competitiveness they enjoyed in the days when, for example, a young defenseman might have gone to the U and been quickly molded by the teaching of Butters. Learning to play at a higher level became easily replaced by sending players away to learn, then recruiting players already at the next level from junior.

When Lucia came in, he was a coach who had adhered to the older-is-better philosophy at Colorado College, with great success. The combination of Lucia not being an M-Man devoted to the old Mariucci theory, and having success with older players, plus the feeling that the Minnesota program was falling behind, led to an alteration. Lucia continued to get commitments from high school players, some as seniors, some even as juniors, but got assurance from most that they would go to the USHL for a year or two first.

Many of the freshmen, sophomores and juniors on the championship team in Lucia's third season had come in as older and more-experienced recruits, but the fact remains that the ringleaders were the seniors, and that crop that included Adam Hauser, John Pohl, Jordan Leopold, Nick Angell, Erik Wendell and Pat O'Leary consisted entirely of players who came to the University as freshmen the year after completing high school. Leopold and Hauser had left high school to play for the USA Hockey Development program in Ann Arbor, but they were "pure freshman" in age coming to college.

Goaltender Adam Hauser was the youngest of the batch. He had left Greenway of Coleraine High School to play at Ann Arbor, so he was considered more experienced when he came to Minnesota. Despite playing more games, Hauser was the youngest of his freshman crop, coming in as an 18-year-old. It was anticipated he would be worked into the lineup slowly, as an alternate to Erik Day, the returning veteran goalie. But during that summer before Hauser's freshman term, Day had his career end with a serious knee injury and surgery.

Not only was Hauser 18 when he started his freshman year, he was still 18 when his freshman season ended. In fact, he was only 21 when he finished his senior year, and didn't turn 22 until May 27, after the trophy had been stashed away. "We had some freshmen who were older than I am," said Hauser.

Not quite, but other teams in the WCHA certainly had freshmen older than Hauser as a senior. And the Gophers had several sophomores who were older. Grant Potulny and Matt Koalska both reached 22 before Hauser, while Nick Anthony hit 22 midway through his junior season, and backup goaltender Justin Johnson was born less than four months after Hauser, even though Johnson was a freshman and Hauser a senior on the same club.

"I could say now that I'm older—even though I'm only 21—but now that I'm older, I have maybe learned a little better as to what goes on," said Hauser. "I had gone to Ann Arbor to play on the U.S. development team my senior year in high school. It was an interesting scenario because a lot of the time when they put you through so much stuff, you hated it to death. But, a lot of times you have to push yourself a little bit further, in order to get to be comfortable in some situations. That's what they were doing. I did like it out there. When I left there, people ask me about it, and I said I knew it was the best experience of my hockey career. You don't get to go play hockey in four different countries on most teams.

"Before my freshman year, I had gotten a call from [assistant] Coach Mike Guentzel that summer," Hauser said. "He said Erik Day had an accident. Erik had many surgeries, but one day he worked out in the weight room and after the workout, he was just walking down the stairs. It was a freaky thing, his knee just broke, going downstairs. So I pull up to the university knowing that it's me and [walk-on] Willie Marvin, and nobody else. Very interesting, I thought."

It got more interesting for Hauser right from the start.

"It was weird for me because I didn't know how they worked things in college hockey," Hauser said. "We started very easy with captain's practices, just scrimmaging. It became very apparent to me there was quite a separation between older and younger guys. I didn't understand it, but apparently there was a very big difference, a pecking order. That's just the way it had always been, for those guys."

Hauser was the target for considerable criticism during his first three years at Minnesota, from fans, media and, earlier, from coaches. Some criticism even carried over to his senior year. It was a long haul for those youthful seniors, but a particularly long road for Hauser from that freshman year.

"As a freshman, I didn't have a clue how to play net," said Hauser. "I had no clue. I was just trying to stop a puck. We had no system, no order, no method to the madness going on in the crease.

"Combine all that with me being a young goaltender who wanted to make everything right, and the only way I knew to do that was to stop everything. When that didn't happen, I started flying off the handle. I got mad—furious—and I was very shaky on the way things were, that freshman year. I didn't know until later on that I had any idea. I didn't know how to save myself. It was madness, in my opinion."

It might have seemed more like madness to Hauser, who always had been an intense but quiet personality. He absorbed the criticism and he suffered, but he suffered in silence mostly.

One outlet he depended on for counsel was Pat Guyer, his high school coach at Greenway of Coleraine. It's ironic that had Hauser stayed at Greenway, the Raiders might have had more state tournament trips, and possibly another title. But even though he pulled out and went to Ann Arbor, his ties back home remain loyal and true. He continued to contact Guyer, who always gave him straightforward guidance for hockey, and life.

"He's always called me," said Guyer. "When he used to give up a goal, he'd bang his stick over the net. That was all part of maturing."

The small-town culture has never left Hauser, and the family connections on the tough, western end of the Iron Range remain. After winning the NCAA title, Hauser turned 22, and turned his attention to the possibility of playing pro hockey, but he still went back home to run a hockey camp in Coleraine for the youngest kids coming up in the Greenway program.

"Adam's mother was our day-care mom, during his freshman, sophomore and junior years," said Guyer.

"He was a tremendous goalie for us. As a freshman, he was 14, a Bantam-age player still. He kept getting better and better because everything he's done, he's thought it through. Even back then, he thought about how and when to go down. He went to Canada to play for the Under-16 U.S. team, and everything was set for him. He was talking then about going to Minnesota. He came back to our team and we played Duluth East and they lit him up. He said, 'I can't stop anything anymore.' I said, 'You can as soon as you start playing for Greenway, and not for the U.S., the Gophers, or Ann Arbor.' He had a goals-against average under 1, and a 97-percent save percentage over the next six games after that."

Hauser, who could isolate himself from most of the close interaction at practice, had a unique perspective. He recalled how the seniors had fallen into a traditional scheme of separating themselves from the younger players. He, like others among the seniors, referred back to future pro Wyatt Smith as an example. When they were freshmen, the captain was Smith, who was from Thief River Falls and had moved to Warroad to play high school hockey.

"Wyatt Smith was a good guy, from what I could tell," said Hauser. "I never conversed with him very much. In warm-ups, I could usually tell where guys were shooting from the angle of the stick or whatnot, certain little things, but I had no idea where Wyatt was shooting. There were a lot of unique things about Wyatt. I admired him a lot, as a player, but it was tough.

Wyatt was very good, almost any day of the week, he was good almost when he wanted to be. I enjoyed playing against Wyatt, because he was always there to play. Stuff was going on, but he was always there to play."

Hauser established a pattern of making spectacular saves almost routinely, but he would then give up a comparatively easy goal, which would sometimes lead to a follow-up flurry of goals. That was true in his first two seasons particularly, and criticism continued through his junior year and even through most of his senior season. The criticism built into a bad rap, sometimes from within comments Hauser heard from Coach Woog, who became more pointed in blaming players in his last years. Woog's cynicism and the criticism in general was hardest for Hauser to handle when he was a freshman, obviously.

"I'll tell you what changed that—Robb Stauber in my second year," said Hauser. "He changed me from being a goaltender just trying to throw a leg out there to stop a puck, to knowing what to look for and how to play. Looking back on it now, my freshman year doesn't seem so much of a nightmare anymore. At the time, it definitely seemed like a nightmare. But now, I realize it was so much of a learning experience. And you know what? It's probably true that without all the stuff that happened that freshman year, maybe I don't think the same way going into the years ahead. Maybe my senior year doesn't happen without my freshman year."

His fellow seniors may not have had the anxiety overload and pressure that Hauser faced, but his comment speaks for all of them, and how they, and their collective character, reached maturity in a hurry, certainly in time for their unforgettable senior year.

Adam Hauser, the youngest senior in college hockey, broke the record for WCHA career victories by beating Maine in the NCAA final.

Jon Waibel signaled his own early-season goal against UMD at Mariucci Arena.

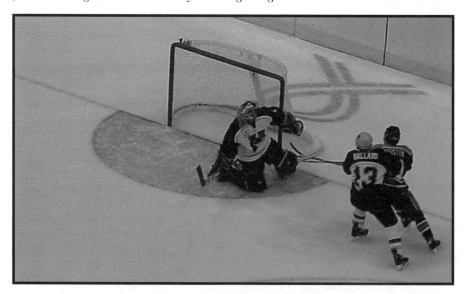

Keith Ballard forces a Black Bear wide while Adam Hauser guards the short side.

Chapter 11

Change overdue

It seemed that Don Lucia must have felt the pressure of heightened expectations in his first season as coach, but he says he didn't. He did, however, almost immediately grasp the realization that some major changes were going to be needed.

"I don't think I've worried about the expectations," Lucia said, "because as a coach, you want to do well for yourself and your players. That's what you're more consumed with and worried about, more than anybody's expectations. When I took the job, I wanted to make it a program the state, the university and everybody would be proud of. Is that winning 20 games, or 25 or 30? I don't know; I've always measured every team I've coached by whether that team reached its potential. That's what I've always looked at.

"Sometimes as coach, you can feel good about finishing .500, because you got the most out of that team. I remember being told that there would be more demands, more things to do. So maybe there were more things to do. So maybe I wasn't as jovial. I wasn't as happy go lucky, just because I was trying to get a handle on the job."

People around the WCHA had listened and muttered for a decade about how the Minnesota program was trying to be the tail that wagged the WCHA dog. Minnesota lobbied for special breaks in years past, such as the assurance it could be scheduled for the fully-paid road trips to Alaska-Anchorage at a time when that also allowed the scheduling of two extra games beyond the NCAA maximum. Minnesota officials would say publicly that because it was an elite program, what was good for the Gophers would be good for college hockey in general. It was the same with cable television revenue, because as a large market, Gopher games could sell ads and be carried statewide. It was a huge recruiting tool, even though it was clearly detrimental to hometown support of St. Cloud State, Minnesota-Duluth, Mankato State, Bemidji State and North Dakota in those cities.

Such manipulations added credence to the perception of arrogance. That feeling was heightened by the fact that every other team seemed to want most to beat the Gophers. So when Lucia came to Minnesota, and changed from shaking his head at such procedures to defending them, people around the WCHA muttered that Lucia had changed from the amiable, humble young coach who had taken Colorado College to incredible heights. They said he seemed to be consumed by what he perceived to be the enormity of the Gopher program.

Lucia disagrees.

"I don't think I changed," he said. "It was the same transition at CC, but it just was a smaller place, and there were not the same expectations. I'm also a big believer that people are envious of this program. I had a coach I won't name who told me, 'Why do you want to take that job? Everybody likes you at CC.' He was insinuating that people wouldn't like me if I took the Minnesota job. You don't change, but I think people look at the job differently. There was a bullseye. It was noticeably different; no matter where you played, what building, everybody wants to beat Minnesota. I didn't have that at CC.

"At CC, Denver was the big rival, but that's it. When I was at CC, Minnesota became a big rivalry for us, but it was because we wanted to beat the best. Here, it didn't matter if we were .500 or the best team in the country. It didn't matter, we were going to get everybody's 'A' game. They wanted to beat us more than anybody else in the country."

"I don't look at myself as changed in any way, whatsoever," Lucia said. "I think people look at you in a different way because of the position. They're not fond of the position, it's not the person."

Ironically, after winning the championship, everyone from the coaches on down through the players showed no trace of the arrogance that once seemed so evident in the faltering years, when the coaching staff and administration were routinely accused of it.

Whether Lucia personally changed—as some of his peers suggest—or whether the image of the carryover smugness of the once-proud program merely left the perception that he had changed—as he suggests—one thing is certain. He found the need to make some changes in the way the team operated, before his first year, after his first year, and after his second year.

"People make so much about coaches, but it's not the Xs and Os that matter most; it's people management," said Lucia. "It's getting your best players to play well, and trying to build a team concept. And having all the players buy into that team concept."

Clearly, that was lacking in recent years. These seniors all recount tales of the divisiveness that was virtually traditional back when they were freshmen, and they all have noted the change.

"Johnny Pohl and those guys were sophomores when I came in, so the guys who were freshmen in my first year and everybody else since then didn't know of any change. Whatever happened the year before I came in.... Those are things I'm not aware of."

But he had heard. Lucia had brought John Hill with him from Colorado College as his first assistant, and retained Mike Guentzel as his second assistant. It didn't take long to discover some evidence that convinced him some changes were necessary.

"One of the things that sticks in my mind, I think it was our first weekend, at home in my first year," said Lucia. "I had talked to the players, then I had to go do a radio wrap-up. Five minutes later, I walked back into the locker room, and there was nobody there. It couldn't have been a half-hour after the game was over, and everybody was already gone. John (Hill) and I were like, 'Where is everybody?' We were used to guys hanging around the locker room, being together, hanging out in the locker room after games, and boom! It was like, how quickly can this place get evacuated? We were stunned. It just reinforced that there was a lack of togetherness. I think that, in the first couple of years, was one of the biggest things we were trying to change."

Such problems are evolutionary more than sudden, and it is not always evident to an existing coaching staff when such problems develop. For a new coach coming in, particularly one who always stressed team unity since his playing days, it was easy to spot. The question then was, how to change it—how to establish togetherness, camaraderie and team unity? If any coach knows how to do that swiftly, he could sell the recipe for enormous profit.

"I think one of the biggest assets we had was that Nate Miller did a great job as captain my first year," said Lucia. "Nate was a really good captain because he was not a superstar, but a role player who bought into everything we tried to do. He was all for it and made things easier. If we'd had a captain who tried to go the other way, and fought us, it would have made it a lot more difficult. Nate was such a good kid, he helped that first year.

"I think Westie—Erik Westrum—did a great job in helping the team become together, too. They had outings together, they started going to movies together. The guys did more things that year, and it continued. Last year, before the school year started, the whole team went up to Matt Koalska's cabin near Alexandria, including the incoming freshmen. Everybody was there. Those are things that never would have happened before."

Koalska, of course, was a freshman himself that year, so it instantly helped the unifying influence of the mass gathering being at his place.

Lucia installed some strict rules, and he limited the access of the media to his players. When the new Mariucci Arena was first built, reporters had free access to the dressing room to interview players after games or before or after practices, and a list of players' home telephone numbers was available to those few media types who followed the team closely enough to want it. The media access to the players was abruptly reduced in Woog's last couple of years, after some of the players had become outspoken in their criticism of Woog.

Lucia tightened things further. The media was never allowed to enter the dressing room, and the only interviews allowed other than on game-days would be on Wednesdays, for a couple of hours before practice, and then only when prearranged by the sports information department. In certain cases, if the need for an interview were urgent enough, an SID staffer would get clearance, then call the player, who would then be allowed to call the reporter, if he chose to.

It's not like there were waves of protests, mainly because there weren't a lot of reporters coming regularly to practices. If there was a noticeable drop in the amount of coverage, and the lack of personality-type stories on players, it still was part of the plan to allow the team total focus on the rebuilding project at hand. It may have had a positive influence on the team, but success was harder to achieve than merely controlling media access.

When the Gophers went 20-19-2, and 13-13-2 in the WCHA in Lucia's first season, an 11-3 surge through January and February was undone by a 3-6 finish. The team was led by Pohl (18-41—59), Westrum (27-26—53), Miller (16-19—35) and Aaron Miskovich (16-16—32).

It wasn't as though everything was perfect, right off. One major disappointment to the state's hockey fans was that Lucia, in his first year, did not raise Dave Spehar to his anticipated place in Gopher hockey history. Once the top goal and point-scorer in Minnesota high school history while starring at Duluth East, Spehar's spectacular play led to heavy media coverage at state tournament time. Lucia suggested that nobody could live up to the massive buildup Spehar got coming out of high school. Some simply said it showed that many high school stars can't make it to the next level.

Spehar had scored over 100 points in both his junior and senior years in high school, including a mind-blowing three straight state tournament hat tricks as a junior, when East whipped state powers Bloomington Jefferson, Edina and Moorhead on the way to the state championship. In college, Spehar led all WCHA freshmen with 20 goals. So much for the transition to college. After scoring 20-17—37 as a freshman, Spehar never became the featured player he might have been. He scored 19-18—37 as a sophomore, then 13-23—36 as a junior. The arrival of Lucia inspired Spehar to get in the best condition of his life for his senior year, to make up for lost time.

But for whatever reason, Spehar never quite fit into Lucia's scheme, although he never complained publicly or to the media, and simply persevered to the end. But after scoring 37, 37 and 36 points for a struggling program in shaky circumstances his first three years, Spehar scored only 9-10—19 as a senior in Lucia's first season. It was a curious finish for a player still considered by some to be the most gifted goal-scorer in Minnesota high school history—scoring the same number of goals all season as he did in the three stunning games at the state tournament five years earlier, when he was a junior at Duluth East.

Goaltender Adam Hauser observed all of that. "It would have been nice if everything would have just clicked immediately when Coach Lucia came in," Hauser said. "Dave Spehar was one example, but I think it was just too late for David to make a point and score a zillion goals as a senior. I do think he enjoyed his senior year more than his other time here. But it would have been cool if he had scored a bunch and been an All-American."

In most other cases, however, the stepping stones to success led to an upward incline. In Lucia's second season, when the Gophers scratched their way to a third-place (18-8-2) record in the league, and battled their way into the NCAA tournament field with a 27-13-2 overall record. Erik Westrum led the team as captain, with a 26-35—61 season, and he cut his penchant for penalty box time from 99 minutes to 84, but the rest of the top scorers were underclassmen. Leopold, from defense, scored 12-37—49, followed by Pohl's 19-26—45, Taffe's 12-23—35, and Grant Potulny's rookie production of 22-11—33, with a team-leading 16 goals coming on the power play.

Having reached the NCAA tournament field for the first time after three failures, the Gophers found a rude finish to their hopes in a 5-4 overtime loss to Maine at the East Regional at Worcester, Mass. It was a tough way to end the season, but the players who returned to school to win the 2001-2002 championship repeatedly brought up that game as perhaps being necessary dues-paying, a cruel ending that would become background incentive in their quest to go beyond merely reaching the NCAA tournament.

Nick Angell's blistering slapshot helped celebrate the WCHA's 50th anniversary—and earned him a belated spot on the Gopher power play.

The Gophers left nobody uncovered against Maine, as Erik Wendell (11), Troy Riddle (21), Keith Ballard (13), Jordan Leopold (3) and Johnny Pohl (9) shielded goalie Adam Hauser.

Chapter 12

Angell finishes on high

Other seniors deserved more headlines, and got them, while Nick Angell took the hard road to a championship ring. He came from regular status as a freshman to less-regular status, to being threatened with being cut from the club, to regaining regular status, and finally winding up playing on the power play at tournament time. Perfect ending for a senior.

A big, always-friendly defenseman, Angell had come from Duluth East with something of a "high-maintenance" tag. He had a booming slapshot from the point but in a way, he ended up acknowledging that he would have been a good example of coach Don Lucia's belief that players should go off after high school to play a year or two of junior hockey, to mature and grow up as much as to develop physically. By the end of his senior year, four years of having to prove and reprove himself to his coaches, Angell had all his struggles washed away by the NCAA championship.

He started off playing quite a bit as a freshman, for coach Doug Woog. Things got a little tougher for him under Don Lucia. While his ability was never questioned, Angell's maturity took a while to catch up to his talent. He was exasperated at some points. But his progression, ultimate contribution to the NCAA title, and his own explanation of it all is the stuff that could make a recruiting brochure sparkle.

It begins with Angell assembling what he calls several important factors to make his decision to choose Minnesota.

"There were a lot of guys at Minnesota I had played with and against in the Maroon and Gold games," Angell said. "Growing up in Duluth, I had watched the Gophers play on Midwest Sports Channel every weekend in Duluth, while UMD games weren't being televised. When I was younger, naturally I watched the UMD games, and whenever the Gophers came to town there was always a little more excitement than for anyone else. Everybody was so anxious to beat the Gophers, and I wanted to be on the team everyone wanted to beat.

"Minnesota was in the Big Ten, a D-1 school, playing in a D-1 facility, and I wanted to go where everything was big time," said Angell.

Angell already had explained the transition to Sanford Hall and a tiny room, from the uncertainty of captain's practices as a freshman to the satisfaction of playing quite a bit as his freshman season went along, including the power play. Then, more uncertainty, right up until the stretch drive of his senior year.

"My four years were not a cakewalk, but I feel pretty prepared to go on into the world," said Angell. "You come in here, and it doesn't take long to switch from being an optimist to a realist. It's not a game, it's a job, and the quicker you realize that, the better off you'll be. We don't just play the season, we have a full-year job, for four years.

"We lost in the regional last year, and we all took a week or two off, then we started working out again. When I was a freshman, there also was a mandatory nine hours of study hall each week that I'd have to go to. Later that got cut down to six hours."

No wonder the players on WCHA teams annually feel the need to take off after the long and grueling season.

"By the time the season is over, you feel like you have to get away," Angell said. "After my sophomore year, I went to Mexico for a week. After my junior year, when we lost to Maine in the NCAA regional, I went to Sweden. While I was over there, I put on 10 pounds.

"When I came back, Coach said, 'Lose 15 pounds, or I'm going to cut you.'

"Now, *there's* an incentive! I lost 20."

Coach Lucia acknowledged that he threatened Angell that his spot on the team was in jeopardy.

"Nick came very close to losing his place on the team," Lucia said. "I like Nick a lot, he's a good kid. I think he was just a little irresponsible, and immature. It got to be an exasperating time last spring, when he had problems academically, but he responded over the summer.

"Basically, we told him if he didn't come in at a certain weight, 208 or 209, he'd be cut. I'm glad it worked out the way it did—glad Nick had a good summer, and came in at good weight. I didn't say a word to him. Everything was up to Nick, in his control.

"It was never about him having the ability to play, just a question of other things keeping him from reaching his potential. If you're going to be there at the end, you've got to have guys who are willing to work hard and do the things necessary on and off the ice to be successful. Nick was a hard worker on the rink every day, but I'm not sure he was the most enthusiastic worker in the weight room or trying to make sure he was in the best physical shape.

"His play would suffer if he got too heavy, so our big challenge was to keep him under 210. He was always better at 208 than at 215. He could shoot the puck, although we worried about him hitting the net."

Angell recalled how tough it was, at the time, to work extra to keep his weight in check.

"When I came back from Sweden, I started working out, hard," Angell said. "It was full-time working out, two hours a day, four days a week, on Monday and Tuesday, then we'd get Wednesday off, then we'd go again on Thursday and Friday, lifting and running sprints.

"My routine this year, once practice started, was to go work out an hour on the stationary bike at Mariucci at 6 a.m., then run back home, shower, and go to class from 9 a.m. until 1:30. There was just time to grab something to eat, then go to practice from 3 until 4:30, and lift weights afterward. I'd get home at 6, eat, do some homework, and sleep."

Lucia chuckled at seeing Nick work out so diligently, and said, 'We figured Nick had spent so much time on the bike he could qualify for the Tour de France."

While Angell would have preferred a less-arduous route, he said he now can see that it all was worth it. He always has been an easy interview, ready and willing to describe game situations or expose his feelings. But he didn't get much chance to do that during his four years.

"I played on the power play as a freshman, then I played some sporadically on the second power play as a sophomore and junior, under Lucia," Angell said.

"After my sophomore year, Gregg Wong wrote in the *St. Paul Pioneer Press* that Doug Meyer and Dan Welch were gone from the team, and that Pat O'Leary and Nick Angell were next," Angell added. "I was pretty embarrassed to have that in the paper, and I went in and asked Lucia about it. He said he didn't know where that came from. I've never said a word to Wong in the three years since then. And Rachel Blount, in the *Minneapolis Star Tribune*? I talked to Rachel once or twice in my four years…when she was doing something special on Jordan and wanted some comment from me."

With Lucia's policy shielding players from open access by the media, Angell's private media flap may have gone unnoticed. But Angell said he appreciated being at Minnesota, even when things looked bleak for him personally.

"I never came close to leaving," Angell said. "Once you're there, you're there. I didn't go to Minnesota just to play hockey. To me it was a four-year deal, and you get exposed to a lot of things. Sometimes times are tough, and you've got to suck it up. It's a good thing I sucked it up. I was on the second power play most of my senior year. But I got a big goal that turned out to be the winner in a 5-4 game at St. Cloud late in the season, and I was on the first power play the rest of the time after that."

He also traced the progression, a routine passing-of-the-torch that potentially could keep the program at the top for years to come.

"With all the great players that come here, you can pencil in the guys, and the freshmen pick up where the seniors left off," Angell said. "We lost Erik Westrum, Steve Senden, Aaron Miskovich and Dylan Mills as seniors last year, and we had eight freshmen to pick up the slack.

"When I was a freshman, there was Pat O'Leary, Jordan Leopold, Mark Nenovich, Johnny Pohl, Erik Wendell, Doug Meyer, Adam Hauser and me. The next year, Matt Koalska, Troy Riddle, Paul Martin and Keith Ballard came in. Because of all the tradition at Minnesota, we always know we're going to be good. But it's not always easy to replace the seniors. It's going to be tough to replace Leopold and Pohl, for example, but it always seems to happen. Look at this year, when we had to replace Westrum."

Erik Westrum was a player who did things his way. He was admired and respected by his teammates for his leadership, just as he was universally disliked by opponents for some occasional stinging hits from behind.

"Westie was a real character. He'd go to bat for you, even if you were the lowest guy on the team," Angell said. "He was playing in the AHL this year, and when we won the title, he drove straight through from Springfield to get back to Minneapolis. He got four speeding tickets on the way, but he kept speeding anyway so he could get here and party with us. He said right away, 'I know I'm not part of this, but you guys are my friends.'"

Angell can still go back to his freshman year, when the hazing of the freshmen made an impression on him and his fellow-rookies, strong enough to cause them to do things differently when they got to be seniors, and took the freshmen under their wings.

"As seniors, we took all the freshmen out to Campus Pizza a couple times, just for camaraderie," Nick said. "I'd pick up the tab...and charge it and send the bill home to my dad."

Angell recalled one other incident to describe the price he and his teammates paid that might have contributed to the championship.

"Before training camp started, we had dryland training," Angell recalled. "One of the things we had to do was to run 200-meter dashes. You had to do 15 of those, right in a row, and they have to be under 31 seconds. That's a pretty good clip. You'd finish running a 200, which is halfway around the track, and you could catch your breath as you'd walk back across the track. Then you'd run another one.

"I'm not a great runner, so I was doing them in 30 or 31 seconds—right on it. After the last one, I gave it everything I had, and I was laying there, practically dead. We were all laying there.

"Coach was there that day, and after we were done with the last one, he said, 'One more.'

"Everybody was puking. We hated it, but it was his way of giving us an extra little push. He'd sneak in one more sprint, just in case we weren't counting. Of course, everybody *was* counting.

"But, when you look back, maybe that's what did it. Maybe that overtime sprint is what got us there in overtime in the final."

Defenseman Judd Stevens prevented UMD's Jon Francisco from threatening goalie Adam Hauser—with the puck, at least.

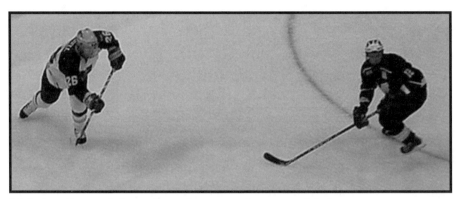

Nick Angell moved the puck on the power play against Michigan.

The Gophers weren't thrilled with Michigan's bad-angle second goal, but they came back to hang on for a 3-2 triumph in the NCAA semifinals.

Chapter 13

Four great years

SOME GOPHERS STRUGGLED during their college hockey careers, some had to work to improve and earn regular status. But Jordan Leopold was very good from his first day on the ice, and when he completed his fourth straight year of excellence on defense, it was only fitting that he was named All-America for the second year in a row and also captured the Hobey Baker Award. Historians might have to go back a few decades, to the days of Johnny Mayasich, to find anyone who came closer to a perfect four-year college career.

As Coach Lucia indicates, a team is only as good as its leaders, and when the leaders are also the team's hardest workers, great things can happen. There is no question that Jordan Leopold and Johnny Pohl were the Gopher leaders.

Ironically, the six championship seniors not only provided optimum leadership, they also represent what might be the youngest crop of seniors that any hockey championship team could possibly have—at least until and unless the NCAA changes the rules about eligibility. Because every team—Minnesota included—now pursues the more sure things of older freshmen, high school graduates who have spent a year or two developing in junior hockey.

But Leopold, Pohl, Adam Hauser, Nick Angell, Erik Wendell and Pat O'Leary all were "true" freshmen, coming to Minnesota the first year after finishing high school. Leopold and Hauser did leave high school to go play for the USA Hockey Development Team in Ann Arbor, Mich., but they were the two youngest players among the Gopher seniors. Hauser, who didn't turn 22 until May 27, 2002, was youngest. Leopold was next, turning 22 on August 3, 2002.

"It's kind of funny, but O'Leary, Pohl, Wendell and Angell are all in my class, but they're all a year older than me," said Leopold. "We have freshmen about the same age as Hauser and me. Grant Potulny was a freshman last year, and he's older than I am. They really understand how the game is played, while younger guys really don't know what to expect. Freshmen can say, we got to listen, and everyone buys into what's being said, but it's different for younger guys.

"Me, Hauser, Pohl, O'Leary, Wendell, Angell—we were all true freshmen when we came in. Really, that's what separates college hockey from major junior. So many guys play a year or two In the USHL, now you've got 21-year-old freshmen. So this year, there are 25-year-old seniors and 21-year-old freshmen. It's a big difference."

The ability to play expanded schedules, with intensive training, in the Ann Arbor program was an obvious benefit, even if it cost Minnesotans the chance to marvel at the skills of Gopher players like Leopold, Hauser, Jon Waibel, Keith Ballard and backup goalie Travis Weber in their peak high school hockey years.

"I was at Armstrong for two years, then I went to the USA Development Program in Ann Arbor for a year," said Leopold. "We played 60 games, and got a little taste of what the next levels would be like, but I got burned out by the end. We had Jeff Jackson, and guys like Greg Cronin, Bob Mancini and others as coaches. Greg Cronin was pretty much my coach. But the whole thing was tough, to take 17-year-olds and treat them the same as college players. We worked out hard, but there was no set plan. I mean, we'd go into the weight room and go to a weight station and say, 'OK, I'll do this 10 times.' Instead of looking up what things we needed to do to help specific development.

"It was good for me to see that side of hockey, but it was nine months of really hard work. I think things have changed around there now, and there's more research on weight training. We were the 'Microscope Kids,' so early in the program. There you were at 17, no mom and dad around. You had to learn how to take care of everything yourself. I definitely got burned out by the end of the year."

He continued to get whatever information he could get while he was at Ann Arbor, and he was aware that the Gophers had faltered.

"Of course, the Gophers used all their NCAA tournament trips as a recruiting tool," Leopold said. "But it was tough for us as freshmen, and as sophomores, because we wanted to make a name for our class. When Lucia came in, it was a breath of fresh air.

"We knew what we had to do, and we knew we had some talent. As for the championship, I think we knew what we could do a year ago. We knew the process and got the right mindset my junior year. We had gotten to the national tournament at least, and that was the first time the Gophers had gotten to the national tournament in six years, or something like that...."

Three, actually, but Jordan had been away....

"...So it was a breath of fresh air when we got to the NCAA my junior year. We lost to Maine, but that was a fun trip. And I think it helped us realize what we could do this year. Our goal was to not only get to the national tournament, but to get a bye in the first round, because that really helps your chances to win it."

That, of course, is precisely the map the Gophers followed on their quest for gold. Among the factors Leopold pointed to was the coaching staff, including new assistant Bob Motzko and veteran Gopher assistant Mike Guentzel.

"Motzko is such a positive guy," said Leopold. "He's not going to harp on you, and he's not negative. He opened our eyes because no matter what he said to us, he would always add, '...but we can do better.' Having him there was great, because he's so upbeat. I mean, Guentzel is upbeat too, and he sweats maroon and gold, but he kind of got frustrated some over the years, I think."

Despite the fact that Leopold won the Hobey, the explosive Gopher offense and the continuing muttering about Hauser's goaltending seemed to dominate the media throughout the championship season, and the defensive corps, as a group, continued to be underrated and overlooked. Coach Lucia, of course, figures the defense was the team's stronghold, and other WCHA coaches felt the same. Not only was their defensive performance consistently solid, but they might have been the best gang in the country at efficiently moving the puck forward and limiting turnovers.

Leopold was prejudiced, but he offered his assessment of his blueline buddies. Leopold was paired with Matt DeMarchi, perhaps the least sophisticated puck-handler, but also the most rugged and aggressive member of the team, who often showd a tendency to overstep his—and assorted referees'—limitations in delivering punishing hits.

"In the middle of the season, when we started giving up goals, you could blame the defense, and the goaltender, and the forwards too," said Leopold. "We didn't blame anybody. We didn't have one guy who thought he was better than another. We ended up winning, and we did it the way we wanted to do it. We changed some things, wanted everybody to get along, be the same, and equal. Sometimes you can have all the talent in the world and it doesn't happen. We really didn't have a weak link.

"I played two and a half years with DeMarchi," said Leopold, "He doesn't worry me, when I remind him to knock it off. When he's out there, he and I had a relationship. It got so Matt could tell you what I'm going to do. He was a big part of our team. We needed what he could give us, and without Matt out there with me, a lot of things might have been a lot different. Basically, he was my little enforcer. He played his role, stayed out of the box and didn't take stupid penalties at the end.

"When we had Westie [Erik Westrum] and DeMarchi out there at the same time, it can worry you a little bit. But I think I had DeMarchi under control enough so he knew to stay out of the box. We had a few conversations about that; it's a role you have to do as captain. It was tough for him, but it was also nice to have him back there. I was always going to watch out for him, and I can't give him enough credit. I told him if he gets in trouble, give me the puck and let me make the mistake.

"Paul Martin has all the skill in the world," added Leopold. "All he has to do is step up and play his game. He'll be paired with DeMarchi next year, I'll bet. He has to take charge. He's such a great athlete, in every sport. It doesn't matter if it's football, baseball, soccer, basketball or whatever, we all want to be on his team. Everybody bought into what was asked. Paul is so laid back, he does whatever you ask him to do. He was only a sophomore, but he had a good freshman year, and he really picked up from where he left off.

"Keith Ballard is another typical offensive defenseman, like Paul or me. That gave us three offensive D, and three other guys who would stay home. Keith was picked in the first round, and he's going to become a player. It's up to him whether he wants to be a good player or become a great player. Definitely, he's got the skating, and the eye, with such great vision of the game, and he's so quick.

"Judd Stevens paired up with Paul most of the year, or with Joey Martin. Stevens didn't know if he was going to play, and almost went back to the USHL. Judd decided to come when Ben Tharp went back to USHL. He wasn't intimidated, played his game, and got better as as the season progressed. We needed that, and it helped Paul's confidence. I roomed with Tallackson the first half of the season, then with Judd after that. He's a good kid, all around. All they talked about was how we were going to do things.

"Nick Angell has got a cannon for a shot, and he played better than ever at the end. He proved himself, and used his shot to his advantage, and put a few on net. He also didn't make any mistakes, that was his downfall before. I think the coaches were sending a message to Nick, that you've got to work to be a player. He got back in shape, ended up being a good player, and went out on top.

"Nick won a state title, then won a national title in college hockey. He's the only guy who won both of them in his last game in both. Johnny and Riddle won states, but they were as juniors. Nick won as senior, both in high school and college. He earned it, and he was a big part of our success, with big plays.

"I think next year will be more of a rebuilding year. They should make the NCAA, but you never know what's going to happen. They've got some good young talent, but it takes a while. Maybe when these juniors are seniors, they could do it again, as long Ballard, Paul Martin and those guys stick around."

Chances are, Leopold will spend his years in pro hockey—and presumably the National Hockey League—keeping track of the Gophers, just as he did when he tried to follow the Gopher hockey fortunes during his year at Ann Arbor before he became a freshman. That's the way it works for those with Gopher Gold running through their souls.

Jordan Leopold paused to ponder a question at the NCAA tournament post-game press conference.

Goaltending give and take: Adam Hauser, who gave out a few chops, admitted that he was doing a bit of acting when Michigan's Eric Nystrom checked him in the crease (above). After a 3-0 lead turned into a 3-2 victory, teammates mobbed Hauser (below) for securing a trip to the final.

Chapter 14

The puck stops here!

IT WAS PRETTY NEAR IMPOSSIBLE to put a barometer out there in the electrified atmosphere of the Xcel Energy Center and try to guess who was the happiest person in the building after Minnesota defeated Maine 5-4 in overtime in the NCAA tournament final. Most likely, it was about a 20,000-way tie. But one of the happiest was Minnesota coach Don Lucia, and a large chunk of the happiness the coach had for his own personal breakthrough NCAA title was dedicated to goaltender Adam Hauser.

"I was really happy for Adam, because Adam is a wonderful young man," said Lucia. "He graduated in four years, he's in the Fellowship of Christian Athletes, he's a good citizen, and a good person. I kept telling people that Adam was judged too young in his career. He was 18 his whole freshman year. How many kids are 21-year-old freshmen? Justin Johnson, I think, is as old as Adam right now, and he's a freshman. Can you imagine if Adam was a freshman this year? Everybody would say he was sensational."

While the true secret to the University of Minnesota's NCAA championship revolved around this mysterious asset called "chemistry," an elusive camaraderie and togetherness that no player or coach seems to be able to really define. The much more obvious asset, always, is to simply look between the pipes. Forwards score goals and defensemen stop foes and advance the puck, but all of that can be futile unless the goaltender comes up with the right saves at the right time.

For the Gophers in 2002—or in 1974, 1976 or 1979, for that matter—Adam Hauser was the young man in the pressure cooker as goaltender. For Hauser, it was more pressure than for most goalies, because he had heard the criticism of giving up "easy goals" since he was a freshman, and it never went away, not even into the Frozen Four. Critics of Hauser will be astonished to learn that by beating Michigan 3-2 in the NCAA semifinals, Hauser tied former Denver University goaltender Ron Grahame with 82 victories, most ever for a WCHA goaltender. When Hauser held on to beat Maine 5-4 in the overtime final, he broke the record. It will take some doing to win more than the 83 Hauser amassed in his four years.

And yet, until the end, he was still considered the Gophers question mark, some said their Achilles heel. Lucia says that he had overcome his own questions about Hauser and made a calculated strategy before the 2001-02 season.

"The biggest challenge all year was to get Adam ready for the end of the year," said Lucia. "Can Adam be the guy? There were question marks, no question. But we felt at the start of the year that our best chance to win the national title was with Adam in the nets. So what could we do to make sure we get him ready by the end? Yeah, he had to feel threatened because we brought in Travis Weber, and he had to overcome that so he could become mentally better.

"I really felt we wouldn't play Adam as much, give him some nights off, and get somebody ready for the following year. People had all these question marks. Then we go into North Dakota, and it was a disaster for Adam. Just a disaster. He had a terrible game where he couldn't get in the way of the puck. Travis went in and played well. But I'd seen Adam play, and I knew that in that first game, we'd only been on ice a week, plus there was the hoopla of the new arena at Grand Forks and all that, so I didn't really feel like that was a big thing."

Hauser indicated that if the whole season played out according to Lucia's master plan, he wasn't aware of it. In fact, he sounded as though he had to continue to prove himself all through the season.

"This year, I knew they were bringing in Travis Weber, and I knew there was going to be some definite competition," Hauser said. "Coach told us from the start he didn't know who our starting goaltender in the playoffs would be. You're going to play as much as you really want to play, he said. So I go out and get pulled in the exhibition game.

"In that first game at North Dakota, the first goal, I saved the puck. I made the move I wanted to make. It was a very hard shot, and I was going to deflect it with my stick into my chest, but it hit my stick and went under my arm, under my glove, instead of into my chest. Everybody was up in arms. Same old thing for me. I think at that point, I started to get sick of things, and I quit thinking. I knew full well that if I put everything together, I could do this thing."

Lucia said his plan worked out, whether by design or necessity. But that first game had to make him wonder if indeed Weber might be ready to jump in as a freshman.

"If somebody stepped forward and played better than Adam, they might have been the one to play, but I really felt our best chance to be successful was Adam. He was a senior, he had played a ton of games, and when Adam was on, we won.

"We started alternating them after the North Dakota game, but that was the plan to begin with—alternate early in the year, then in that tough, six-game stretch of Michigan-Michigan State, St. Cloud and Denver, Adam played all six of those. And played well. We broke for Christmas time, and got back into alternating, and we got Travis and Justin Johnson in there. Adam had a bad game against Wisconsin in Madison, but I came back with him the next night. I wanted to show him we had faith in him.

"In February, he tweaked his ankle and couldn't play the first night against CC, but otherwise, he played every game thereafter. But it was what we wanted. He didn't have to play every night, or have the mental burden of playing every night. So he was fresher at the end. I felt going into the NCAA playoffs that if Adam could stop nine out of every 10 shots, we were going to win that game. And he did that, throughout the NCAA tournament."

Hauser seemed like an introverted, complex personality when he came in as a freshman and was thrust into regular duty on a team that was in the process of coming apart. Instead, he is refreshingly straightforward—candid, sensitive to the criticism but always harder on himself, and someone who was reluctant to open up to his teammates, right up until the finish.

"From a team perspective, I try not to think at all about future stuff," Hauser said. "It gets really hard. You end up complicating things so much for yourself, way more than you really have to. If the focus is on taking one day at a time, one practice at a time, one game at a time—it's a cliché, but there's a reason why it's become a cliché."

Sometimes the criticism got harsh in his freshman year, but he said he had no problem with Doug Woog as coach, despite the difficulties he had personally.

"Things were OK, but it's a very complicated thing," Hauser said. "Personally, I have difficulty with coaches who don't know goaltending. It's kind of a general thing, I just have a hard time with head coaches who weren't goalies. This has nothing to do with any of the coaches I've had on the way up, but Jeff Jackson, who coached me at Ann Arbor, was a goaltender. At Ann Arbor, he taught me a lot about goaltending. But coaches in general have a hard time with goaltenders. I think it's because it's a very misunderstood position. Robbie Stauber and I talk about it a lot. If you're not a goalie, or have never been in the past, then you'll never know.

"I was 18 as a freshman, for my whole freshman year. My birthday is May 27, 1980, so I turned 19 after my freshman year was over. I was only 21 my whole senior year. Going back to high school, I was 14 when I first started playing for Greenway. In my freshman year back then, it was funny, people would tell me that I was closer in age to guys playing Peewee than guys in high school. That was weird."

One fascinating aspect of Hauser's game is that he seems to stop the toughest shots, but occasionally a seemingly easy goal eludes him. It used to be, those goals would seem to frustrate him and make him susceptible to allowing more goals. Hauser heard all the accusations.

"If I stop all the ones nobody is going to question me on, and I let in a few of the shaky ones, let's reverse it," Hauser said. "Let's stop all the ones I'm supposed to stop and let in all the ones nobody is going to question me on. I'm convinced that way we'd lose 12-1.

"I let in a few shaky ones, but that changed over four years. You've got to look at how the game was played. There were so many breakaways, 2-on-0s and 2-on-1s the first two years, then the third and fourth year, it changes. The defensive corps gets better. More skill there, bigger guys, more physical, smarter guys, and things change. Whether it was me or anyone else, any goaltender would have an easier time of it with better defensemen."

As for Woog, Hauser said: "Yeah, he gave me a pat on the back now and then. He talked about Robbie Stauber a lot. I heard the stories of how Robbie Stauber stopped eight breakaways in the third period, or something like that, against Wisconsin to save the day."

When Lucia took over, he hired Stauber as part-time goaltending coach, and he became mentor and close confidante to Hauser. The effect started to show when Hauser was a sophomore and junior, and reached full bloom by the time he was a senior. Lucia says he brought in Stauber for some specific reasons. "Robb is a great teacher, and he had Adam work on the things he thought would be important for him," Lucia said.

"It wasn't just Robbie Stauber, it was Coach Lucia as well," Hauser said. "He also wanted consistency from his goaltender, and he had expressed that to me. There was some other stuff going on. He didn't think I spent enough time with the guys, and said I should try to do that more. I think some of the difficulties I had go back to the fact that…coaches don't always understand goaltenders."

Hauser agreed that not all the players thrived immediately on Lucia's coaching, and some didn't get any tangible benefits.

"I noticed a change in Donnie over his three years at Minnesota, too," Hauser said. "At first, he wanted to show who was boss. That's a good thing. You have to display that you are in control and you're going to do things your way. At the same time, the players were looking for consistency. It was a learning experience for everyone. For *everyone*. It was a better situation, but not a great year."

The goaltending structure in practice did change dramatically for Hauser.

"Bob Mason was there as goalie coach my freshman year, and I loved Mase," Hauser said. "I think his hands were tied. There was only so much he could do. He had very limited time with me. Robbie was able to be there almost every day. I felt a lot better about my game, and I had a reason for doing a lot of stuff. There were some interesting developments the previous year that I was able to learn from and formulate a way of playing. It was great. I was still holding a lot of stuff from my sophomore year. Although I felt my sophomore year was a pretty good year, I think I was being too selfish. A lot of time I was thinking too much. There was a lot of stuff I was thinking. The numbers were better, but I still don't think the jump from my sophomore to my junior year was as good as I wanted it to be. That kind of woke me up."

Coach Lucia, and Hauser's high school coach, Pat Guyer at Greenway of Coleraine, both tried to prod Hauser to loosen up, and interact more with his teammates, before his senior year.

"Adam has always been more of a loner," said Lucia. "That's one of the things we tried to stress: 'Adam, be with your teammates more. Go play golf with them. I understand you don't drink, but do things, go to a party for just an hour or two, go bowling, go to a movie, go to lunch—do things with your teammates.' Those are part of the dynamics we were trying to do in team-building. Because they've got to want to play for you, too."

The opening game up at North Dakota, when the plush Ralph Engelstad Arena was unveiled for an exhibition between North Dakota and the Gophers, was painful for Hauser. And there was more discomfort as the season went on.

"I tried not to read the papers, during my first three years here, but I still did," Hauser said. "After that game, I *quit* reading the papers. I wasn't watching news programs. Nothing. When we went up to North Dakota for the series later on, I had expected to play one of the two games. We'd been splitting up until that point. My feeling was, I don't care which one, just get me in one of the games. But I wasn't slated to play either one of them, I guess. They brought Justin Johnson up and he played the first game, and we won, so they started him again Saturday. But they pulled Justin early on in the second period. So I go in and make the saves I was supposed to make. Then everybody was coming back to me and saying how I was the greatest. What can you do?"

Goalies know exactly how the puck got by, but to Hauser, dwelling on them was not productive.

"You look at the NHL playoffs, when Detroit scored 10 goals in the seventh game against Colorado on Patrick Roy, who some people think is the best goalie in the world," Hauser said. "I wasn't happy with the announcing. They made it sound like he was throwing the game. I didn't expect anything different from the announcers. It just shows you how much everyone looks at a goaltender.

"I get uncomfortable when I talk about goals. I really do," he said. "Because, there's obviously a way that a goalie could stop every goal that goes in. The reason each goal goes in is because the goalie didn't stop it. And there's a way the goalie could have gotten there to stop it. That's the way I thought of it, really hard-core in the past. I thought that I had to be there for every single goal. As I've grown a little bit older now, I know that stuff is going to happen."

After playing at Ann Arbor, does the concept of playing a year or two of junior make sense?

"I was never a big fan of players playing eight years or whatever in the USHL and then coming into college hockey," Hauser said. "But you know what? It matters. Wade Dubielewicz was a junior at Denver my senior year, and everybody was all ga-ga over him because he's a good goaltender. But he's what—23? He was 23 in his junior year and I didn't turn 22 until after my senior year was over. It matters how old you are."

Some of the harsh things he heard came from the stands, but some came from Coach Doug Woog, too, who was going through his own personal dilemmas as the program came apart under him. Sometimes—too often—that frustration boiled over to personalized criticism of players, in front of other players. Some of them took it and bristled, some got tougher, but some, like the youngest player on the team, a solid and sensitive Christian from Bovey, were nearly shattered by it.

Hauser doesn't talk about that very much in retrospect, but he withdrew a lot in his early days, and depended on phone calls home to Pat Guyer, his high school coach at Greenway of Coleraine. Greenway might have had another state tournament run or two had Hauser stayed in high school instead of going to Ann Arbor. But there was no bitterness. In fact, Guyer remained Hauser's main confidante through his college days, as a constant source of guidance.

"When he was a freshman, he'd call me every week and we'd always have good long talks," recalled Guyer, who also runs the arena in Coleraine, where Hauser ran a youth hockey camp in the summer after he'd won the NCAA title and graduated. "Adam loves to get out there working with kids. He's at his best doing that, and he's always done it. He ran our Mites program [ages 5-8] for two years when he was playing for us, before he went to Ann Arbor. We still bring him back up here to run the camp every summer.

Whenever Hauser called, Guyer was there for him, for long, philosophical discussions, and he noticed the advancing maturity. "Last summer, before his senior year, I told him to get more involved with his teammates," Guyer said. "I told him to take a freshman and ask him to go out for lunch or something. And then do it with the sophomores.

"I'll tell you how much he matured," Guyer added. "He called me three times at the end of the season, but I wouldn't return his calls. He was going too good, and I was afraid I would have screwed it up."

It's not like Hauser needed any further confidence boosting, or guidance, by that point. In fact, Stauber said he, too, had pretty much left Hauser to stay in his own "zone."

"He was so great in the NCAA regional, and great in the Frozen Four," said Stauber, that night at Xcel Energy Center. "He was sharp, but calm. I haven't said a word to him for three weeks. The last thing I said to him was, 'Just think of some of your best games, where you were calm, and duplicate it.'"

Easier said than done, but it was something Hauser accomplished in those final weeks. And he grew to one more higher level—literally—off the ice.

"After the NCAA final, he called me," said Guyer. "He said he had gone with a lot of the guys when they all went over to the Library, a joint on campus. He said Jordan and Pohl were up on the bar, celebrating. Then he said, 'I got up there too, and I was up there for 45 minutes, leading cheers.' "

It took the full four years, but finally all the criticism and painful moments for Adam Hauser were replaced by a record number of goaltending victories, an NCAA championship ring, and a rightful place up on the stage where the team leaders belonged.

Johnny Pohl was an All-American at both ends of the rink: He went to the net to score enough points (27-52—79) to lead the nation (above), and he also went to his own net to prevent Maine from scoring in the NCAA final (below).

Chapter 15

The Pohl chronicles

For all four of his years, Johnny Pohl was simply too good to be true. He never complained when he wasn't in the lineup; he just figured he'd better work harder and do things better. He never protested when he played wing, instead of his natural center position. To talk to Johnny Pohl, you'd think nothing was ever out of place, and that everything happened for a reason.

If you read the requisites for being voted winner of the Hobey Baker Memorial Award as the best player in college hockey, it sounds like a biographical sketch of Johnny Pohl. Yet he never complained about being overlooked for the award—and inexplicably being ignored when the 10 finalists were named.

"Hobey? No, I didn't feel slighted at all," said Pohl. "The Hobey goes to the most talented and best player in college hockey. Jordan Leopold is as skilled and polished a player as there could possibly be. There's no defenseman better in college hockey. On top of that, he's a great leader. I knew all year I couldn't win it. You can't win the Hobey if you're not the best player on your own team.

Part of Pohl's gift is that he is as humble as he is skilled, all of which contributes to his ability as an over-achieving leader, same as he was when he singlehandedly put Red Wing on the Minnesota state high school map.

It's up to others to praise Pohl, and they do. "I can't believe Johnny wasn't at least a finalist for the Hobey," said Leopold, a two-time All-America.

Coach Don Lucia put it best when he said Pohl was as fine a person as he had been around, and the hardest working player he had ever coached, in 22 years. And in the championship year, Lucia's praise was worth repeating: "As much as anybody, he put the team on his back in January and February and lifted them up to this level."

In high school, Pohl was named all-state four times, and led Red Wing to the state Class A title in 1997, captivating the entire state with his playmaking skills. At Minnesota, he didn't break in with a burst, but had to pick his way through a veteran squad, even though it was seeking exactly what he could provide. Still, he scored 7 goals, 10 assists for 17 points as a freshman. When Lucia replaced Doug Woog as coach, Pohl's talents were pushed more to the forefront. He scored 18-41—59 as a sophomore, and 19-26—45 as a junior playing with a broken wrist. As a senior, when it was time to hoist the whole team on his broad shoulders, Pohl never flinched, and wound up with 27-52—79 for stats as the top scorer in the nation.

That's exceptional progression, but it still overlooks the facts of what he did under pressure. He got an assist when the Gophers built a 3-0 lead against Michigan and held on for a 3-2 victory over Michigan in the Frozen Four semifinals. And he got a goal, then assisted on the last-second equalizer, as well as the overtime game-winner, in the 5-4 championship victory against Maine. He also took almost every important faceoff against Maine, just as he did whenever an important game was on the line.

A month after the NCAA tournament and the end of his college career, Pohl could be found working out at Mariucci Arena—any day, and every day. He lifted weights and pedaled stationary bikes, and hopped to a plyometric tune, long after his teammates had taken off for lunch or a round of golf. And when it seemed that the place was deserted, a check inside the arena would find Pohl running a series of timed sprints. His new objective was to ready himself for an NHL tryout. He had been drafted by the St. Louis Blues, where the watchful eye of former Gopher star and Blues scout Mike Antonovich considered him a sure thing.

As an All-America, national scoring champion and NCAA ring bearer, it must have seemed a long time ago for Pohl to look back at his frustrating freshman year. Should we be surprised that he took positive energy from it all?

"When I came here, I just wanted to play," said Pohl. "I thought the team would be great, and just to be a part of it would be great. Then three games into my first year, I was a healthy scratch. That hurt a lot. It was the first time it had ever happened to me. I thought I'd be playing, but I didn't get the call. I didn't come to sit on the bench.

"The rest of the year, my goal was just to get in the lineup and try to contribute. I kind of found a role as third or fourth line center. I wasn't on the power play or penalty kill. I just tried to get better every day in practice. I played with Erik Wendell and Stuart Senden, and by the end of the year, we had a pretty good line. We took it to teams, and I think we almost had the highest plus-minus on the team. Even as a freshman, I felt pretty confident I could take the next step.

"Coach Woog ranked our players as 1-2-3. When I was recruited, I was told I would be a 2 as a freshman, but after that, I'd be a 1, which means the chance to play power play, penalty kill and all. I'd say I was more of a 3 than a 2 my freshman year, but I don't have any regrets. I think it made me appreciate it more later. As much as I would have loved to be a 1 as a freshman, I think I learned more."

Then came the coaching change. After the team floundered, Don Lucia was brought in to replace Woog.

"The adjustment went as smoothly as it could have gone," said Pohl. "My dad told me when I went to Minnesota that coach Woog might not be there all four years. I understood. I knew he had been there 15 or16 years, and he was getting a little older. But I had confidence in the program that whoever they brought in would be a great coach. This is *the* place to coach and every coach would love to coach here.

"I remember the first meeting we had with Coach Lucia. He was very professional, very down to earth. He seemed to care about us as players. That helped a lot. He never put any pressure on us as players.

"I thought my sophomore year went pretty well. Brad Arnett, our strength coach, I think really cared about me as a person and wanted me to get better. I stayed up here and worked hard on my skating all summer. I played with Erik Westrum on a line. We had a pretty good first weekend, and I think coach had some faith in me. I think I was put into a different role, on power plays, killing penalties. Instead of 9 or 10 minutes a game, I was playing 20-21 minutes. After a year of not playing much, I was fortunate to be playing more. I didn't want to go back."

Still, the team was destined to miss the NCAA circus for the third straight year. But Pohl understood the building process, and the adjustment time to the new coaching rules.

"We had a brutal schedule that year," Pohl said. "We were at Maine, hosted Boston College and North Dakota, then went to Wisconsin and Colorado College. I don't know if anyone ever had that tough of a schedule, but it really helped us. Especially our younger players. By the end of the year we started to really play well.

"Since Coach Lucia came in, everything has been much more organized. Every Monday was the same, every Tuesday pretty much the same. You got to know what to expect every day. And we were *always* fresh for the weekend. Coach Lucia is very relaxed, a lot more businesslike, and there is not much yelling and screaming. If you make a mistake, he's going to tell you about it. Things were much more organized, too, although that might be kind of unfair for me to say it because for any freshman, your freshman year is just a blur."

Does the NCAA title compare to winning the state high school crown?

"As a high school player," Pohl recalled, "anything less than a state tournament was pretty much a disappointment. I remember getting e-mails from friends, cousins, people saying 'wouldn't it be cool to end it with national title?' I honestly never really thought about it.

"The thought that really scared me the most, was playing my last game. At some point, I knew I was going to play my last game as a Gopher. I was more afraid of that day, and having it maybe be a loss....

"Instead, we're the only team in the country that ended the season with a win. In terms of expectations, the sky was the limit, but we never really talked about the national title. Coach Lucia told us we were going to try to build toward the end of the season. Our objective was to get better every game, and try to be our best in March. I think our guys were great. Nobody complained all year if they weren't playing where they wanted. There were times when we struggled, and maybe we were trying something out that didn't work. But it all worked out in the end."

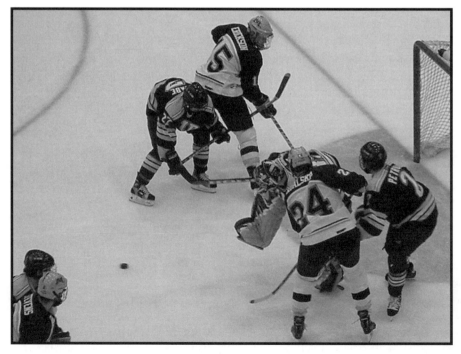

Matt Koalska and Mike Erickson positioned themselves for a rebound.

Chapter 16

Preview of payback

JOHNNY POHL—All-America, former Mr. Hockey, future pro, and historian supreme—can readily recount the sequence of key goals, big games and significant happenings throughout the 2001-02 season that led up to Minnesota's 2002 NCAA championship. But everybody connected with Gopher hockey, except the incoming freshmen, can trace the first "big game" that was truly pivotal to the Gopher championship. And it didn't even happen in the championship season. No, it ended the previous season.

Remember that the 2000-01 season ended with the Gophers qualified to return to the NCAA tournament's select 12-team field after missing three straight years. It was almost the same cast of characters, but it was a strange and enigmatic team that rose and fell in ways that could mystify even coach Don Lucia. Lucia's second year at the helm meant the Gophers were catching on to his philosophies. It looked impressive when Minnesota came out of the chute with a 6-0-1 start, and were in position to take a run at the league title right up until the last two weekends. Equally as surprising, the Gophers ended the regular season by losing three of their last four league games, two of them to St. Cloud State—a costly sweep because Minnesota wound up third, only two points behind St. Cloud State and four points off North Dakota's championship pace.

The Gophers didn't exactly go roaring into the NCAA tournament, either, because after sweeping Michigan Tech to open the WCHA playoffs, they lost 3-0 to St. Cloud State in the semifinals, then fell 5-4 to Colorado College in the third-place game.

Once in the NCAA field, it's sudden-death: lose and turn in the equipment. When Minnesota was selected, it was to head east, to the East Regional at the Centrum in Worcester, Mass., where the opponent would be Maine, the runner-up in Hockey East, and another at-large pick.

This was a chance to put things back in order, to recapture the impressive upside shown by the Gophers much of the season, and to erase the sputtering conclusion. The enthusiasm was widespread by the players, who were making their return to the NCAA territory after missing the previous three years. For captain Erik Westrum, it meant a chance at final validation, but it was no less important to the other seniors—as well as to the herd of underclassmen who had always thought they belonged in the elite NCAA field.

But nobody could have anticipated the incredible parallels in that East Regional game and what would occur just over a year later at the Xcel Energy Center in Saint Paul. Consider, for example, that the starting goaltenders were Adam Hauser for Minnesota and Matt Yeats of Maine, a pair of juniors who would run into each other again a year later. Or that Don Lucia was trying to raise Minnesota's standards while having never beaten a Maine team being coached by Shawn Walsh, who had started the Black Bear program 17 years earlier, and was battling courageously against cancer. Who could have guessed that Walsh would lose his life to cancer just before the 2001-02 season began, and the Black Bears would go all the way to the title game with a Walsh jersey on the bench as tribute to their inspirational leader?

Beyond that, however, was the game itself, which unfolded with eerie similarities to the 2002 title game. Only in mirror-image reversal.

Johnny Pohl was at right wing with the mercurial Westrum at center and Grant Potulny, then a freshman, at left wing. That line arrangement looks curious in retrospect, because it meant Lucia was putting one of the best centermen in state, school and league history at wing. Nonetheless, there he was, scoring on a rebound to open the game on a power play, after Westrum, predictably, had shot from the right boards, and Potulny, equally predictably, had deflected the shot on goal.

The 1-0 lead stood until 6 seconds remained in the first period. Actually, 5.6 seconds. At that moment, Tom Reimann sent an outlet pass to Robert Liscak, who fed Todd Jackson speeding up the right boards. Jackson raced around the Gopher defense with enough velocity to cut behind them and hold the puck until he crossed the goal-mouth and beat Hauser with a backhander. Minnesota had outshot Maine 14-7 but the game stood 1-1.

In the second period, Pohl pounced on a broken outlet play at the Maine blue line and curled to the left boards as Potulny drove toward the net, taking defenders with him. Pohl then passed back toward the blue line where Westrum slammed a one-timer that Potulny deftly tipped past Yeats and just inside the left pipe for a 2-1 Minnesota lead at 8:44. But Maine already had elevated its play, after being outplayed for one period.

Two minutes after Potulny's tip-in goal, Lucas Lawson skated up the right side on what looked like a harmless 2-on-2—actually 2-on-3 if Erik Wendell could catch Lawson on the backcheck. The play lost its harmless status abruptly, when senior defenseman Dylan Mills cut across to help freshman Paul Martin handle the puck-carrier, just as the puck slid through all of them. Lawson, cutting sharply toward the net and one stride ahead of Wendell, pounced on the puck with just enough time to shift to his forehand and score for a 2-2 tie.

Early in the third period, Gopher sophomore defenseman Matt DeMarchi readied himself to be checked by bringing his arms up, and he flattened Liscak with an elbow to the head for a penalty at 2:44. It took only 14 seconds for Maine to take the lead on the power play, when Reimann's shot from the left point was blocked, but the puck went right to Doug Janik at center-point. Janik, Maine's captain, fired a quick shot that glanced in off the left pipe to make it 3-2.

But it was Janik who was called for a slashing penalty at 6:03, and Minnesota countered for another power-play goal. This time Jordan Leopold rushed into the Maine zone, peeled back and passed to the right point, where Mills cut loose. Sure enough, there was Potulny battling for position in front of the net, and he got his stick on the missile to deflect it past Yeats's glove and into the upper right corner at 7:07.

A couple minutes after that, Pohl saw traffic in front and shot from the right boards. Westrum tipped the shot, which hit Yeats's arm, just above the glove. The puck popped up, and as it descended beyond the goalie, Westrum swatted at it and sent a waist-high shot tumbling into the cage.

Minnesota led again, 4-3, and the Gophers played with great poise the rest of the way, pressing on a power play, then killing a couple penalties. As the clock showed 1:00 remaining, and Yeats scurrying to the bench for a sixth attacker, Reimann and Paul Martin jockeyed for position in front of the Minnesota goal. Reimann went down, and the whistle blew. To the amazement of Martin and the Gophers, Martin was penalized for slashing on the play. Repeated video replays failed to disclose anything resembling any infraction, and particularly a slash, but the Black Bears went on the power play with 58.4 seconds remaining in the third period.

Coach Walsh kept Yeats on the bench for a 6-on-4 edge, but Hauser and the Gophers did a very efficient job of defusing the Maine attackers, blocking shots, clearing the zone and scrambling to cover in front. With 5 seconds remaining, Francis Dalton cut loose with a shot from the right point. It was blocked, as Hauser dropped to the ice. The rebound came out on the left side, as the attackers view the goal, right on the stick of Marty Kariya. But with Hauser still in the way, Kariya, who is right-handed but was stationed on the left, passed, neatly, across the crease instead of ramming a hasty shot, and Michael Schutte, a left-handed shooter playing on the right edge of the crease, had an easy tap for the tying goal.

Only 2.7 seconds remained, and the Black Bears had tied the game 4-4 on a power play, which was gained by a controversial penalty call. Anything sound familiar yet?

Overtime opened with Maine's Matthias Trattnig penalized at 0:37 for running DeMarchi from behind into the boards. It was called cross-checking. The Gophers put on some pressure, carrying beyond the power play. Junior Pat O'Leary fed a great pass to freshman Jon Waibel, breaking up the slot, but Yeats came out and the play just missed. Pohl then broke in alone from the blue line, pulled the puck back and snapped a 10-foot wrist shot for the open right side of the net, but Yeats snatched it with a quick glove. Troy Riddle, another freshman, sprinted up the right side and fed a crisp pass across the slot, where big Nick Angell was coming hard. Angell shot off the pass, but Yeats made a huge save. A defenseman crashed into his own goal, taking it off the posts at just the right moment to nullify a Jeff Taffe attempt at a rebound into the open net.

Taffe and O'Leary had a couple more great scoring chances, but the Black Bears, and Yeats, who made 40 saves as Minnesota outshot Maine 44-39, held on.

At the other end, Hauser had less work, and he got away with an indiscretion when he doubled up Lawson with a thump of his big stick to the Maine forward's midsection. But there was no call. Imagine that, a goaltender chopping an attacking forward and getting away with it!

But at 13:04 of overtime, the speedy Todd Jackson raced up the right side against two retreating defensemen and the backchecking O'Leary. Unable to turn the corner this time, Jackson flung a shot on goal, as the big O'Leary stopped in the slot and pivoted to take on any arriving attackers. Hauser blocked the shot, but the rebound squirted straight out. Hauser stepped out after it, but he had to reach his stick in amid O'Leary's skated to pull the puck free, then he sent a clearing pass off toward the left corner.

In a flash, Robert Liscak had cut to that spot and blocked the clearing attempt, quickly flipping the puck back on goal and into the net.

That concluded quite a day at the Centrum. Colorado College had beaten St. Lawrence in two overtimes in the first game, for the right to advance to play North Dakota in the quarterfinals. Then Maine had pulled off an incredible overtime victory over Minnesota in the second game, for the right to advance to face Boston College in the other East Regional quarterfinal.

As it turned out, those two victories might have taken too much out of both winners, because North Dakota and Boston College both won to advance to the Frozen Four, where BC beat the Fighting Sioux in the championship game. The BC victory over Maine was not without controversy, as Maine coach Shawn Walsh was thrown out after a call by referee Steve Piotrowski. Because his courageous battle with cancer ended in his untimely death just before the 2001-02 season started, that turned out to be Walsh's final game as Maine coach, just as Maine's victory over Minnesota was Walsh's final coaching victory.

Meanwhile, Westrum, Mills and the other Gopher seniors went on with their lives, while the returnees all came back with a different focus for the summer workouts, and for the fall of 2001.

"We lost to Maine, but that was a fun trip to Worcester," said Jordan Leopold. "They scored in the closing seconds and beat us in overtime—the exact reversal of what happened when we played Maine in the championship game this year. Losing that game to Maine wasn't fun, and it still hurts. But in a way, it was a springboard to what we knew we could do this year. Our goal was to not only get to the national tournament, but to get a bye in the first round, because that really helps your chances to win it."

Matt Koalska, only a freshman on that 2000-01 team, offered more perspective. "As soon as we lost to Maine last year, we knew we'd be good," said Koalska. "We had good guys coming back, and good guys coming in."

No longer were they a bunch of promising players who wondered if they could ever get to the NCAA tournament. The Maine game made them realize that they not only could get there, but once there, they could do more. The parallels are inevitable—a goal in the final seconds of regulation, a controversial penalty call, and a victory in overtime.

More fodder for the 2002 Frozen Four to come.

Huge scoreboard, fabulous seats, all the amenities, plus only championship banners, give the new Ralph Engelstad Arena at North Dakota everything—except a dedication-game victory.

Freshman goalie Travis Weber gained experience in relief to win the opener at North Dakota.

Chapter 17

Only an exhibition

EVERYBODY WAS IMPRESSED with the ingredients that went into the 2001-02 championship team, even though at the start of the season, nobody could have envisioned quite how the whole thing might come together. The lesson learned against Maine in the 2001 East Regional, the obviously stirring leadership from the seniors, and the unprecedented work-ethic through the long, hot summer of working out contributed to a positive outlook, but nothing was obvious.

One reason for a lack of optimism was that at the very top of the schedule loomed a date at Grand Forks, N.D., an October 5 exhibition game against North Dakota. The Fighting Sioux had commanded complete respect from the whole country, particularly the WCHA, and maybe *most* specifically Minnesota's players, because they had proven themselves to be perhaps the nation's most elite hockey program for the previous five seasons. The Sioux won three straight WCHA titles when Dean Blais first took over as coach, then after dropping to second for a year, they reassumed the top spot in 2000-01. Four championships out of five, with NCAA titles thrown in there in 1997 and 2000 and a runner-up NCAA finish in 2001.

Beyond that, the reason for an exhibition game against its most traditional rival made sense for North Dakota, because it would be the official dedication game at the spectacular new $100-million Ralph Engelstad Arena. It became easily the most spectacular hockey facility in the world. To start with, there is $1 million in bricks alone, 100,000 square feet of Italian granite, 3.2 miles of brass inlays, cherry wood armrests on all of the 11,500 seats, there are 14 locker rooms, 300 television sets for those caught in the concourse (or press box), a $2 million Daktronic scoreboard, and a second ice sheet of Olympic size for practices whenever the Sioux are heading away to play on the bigger sheets at places such as Minnesota, Wisconsin, Anchorage or St. Cloud.

The home dressing room has cherry wood lockers, and training areas that include an underwater treadmill, a spring-mounted wood floor to offer resilience and cut down on workout injuries, a sauna and hot tub large enough for the entire team. Fans can head up to their 48 luxury suites or to two cherry-wood-lined club rooms by four escalators, five elevators, or, if they're feeling primitive, by climbing some staircases, looking up at enormous murals of historical scenes from Fighting Sioux games past.

Ralph Engelstad, a former Sioux goaltender from Thief River Falls, worked in construction and started his own company in Grand Forks, then took a chance on investing in some real estate in Las Vegas, back in the early 1960s. He later sold a chunk of land to Howard Hughes, reinvested in more land and built the Imperial Palace in 1979, which later was expanded to become the largest privately-owned hotel in the world with over 2,600 rooms. He also used his increasing wealth to help build a NASCAR race track near Las Vegas and other facilities. But he never lost his dedication to the University of North Dakota, and he has continued to donate enormous sums to help build campus facilities.

The previous hockey arena was a near-perfect facility, but the new facility staggers the imagination. Mariucci Arena is a fantastic place to watch a hockey game, and the Xcel Center in Saint Paul is nearly perfect. Engelstad Arena is like a slightly downsized Xcel Center, with polished granite and marble replacing cement slab floors, and cherry wood, brass inlays and leather embellishing almost every surface. The Fighting Sioux logo also is embossed nearly everywhere, including on the backrests of every seat. That, too, is a focal point of Engelstad's determination.

Activists have been traveling all over the country trying to pressure schools and professional teams to change what can be construed as derogatory. While officials at the University of North Dakota had always taken care to consult with regional Native American officials, and had gotten general reassurance that the majority felt honored by the "Fighting Sioux" tribute, the activists had made their move and gotten school officials to consider changing names. Engelstad balked. He also insisted that the name Fighting Sioux be retained, or he would halt production on the new facility and, because of his unique arrangement for ownership of the land, he would leave it half-done and never again donate to North Dakota's welfare.

School officials fell into line supporting Engelstad and the continuation of the name. When activists challenged the team logo in the past, the proud Native American head festooned with feathers was dropped for a caricature outline of a headdress-bedecked head. A change to a more realistic head with feathers had been ordered, and when some activists challenged it, they were stopped cold. Bennett Brien had been hired to create the new symbol. Brien is a Native American artist from Belcourt, N.D., who holds a Master of Fine Arts degree from the University of North Dakota. He had reasons for every facet of the symbolic new logo, and Engelstad proudly commanded that it be embossed everywhere, throughout the arena.

With the arena completed, and the ceremonial game sure to attract national attention—Sports Illustrated came, but pretty much wrote off the new facility with a politically-correct attack on Ralph Engelstad that was far more intense than anything that wonderful magazine has ever attempted on a higher-profile target such as the Washington "Redskins." The Gophers spent one week of practice and took their hopeful outfit to Grand Forks to challenge the WCHA's defending champions. Then they had to endure the pregame laser light show, speeches by dignitaries that included Ralph Engelstad himself, and a large and relatively goofy crowd of 11,690—the largest crowd ever to watch a hockey game in the state of North Dakota, obviously.

The game was a test for goaltenders, because Adam Hauser was the senior Gopher, and Andy Kollar finally was getting his senior year in the spotlight at North Dakota, after playing very well as backup and alternate behind the brilliant but graduated Karl Goehring for three years. Kollar's position was secure as the anchor to what was assumed would be yet another Sioux run at WCHA and NCAA laurels.

Then the puck dropped, and it was a nightmare for any goaltender.

Dakota's Chad Mazurak beat Hauser on a slapshot from left point at 6:00, but freshman Mike Erickson scored with a backhander at 6:30 to tie it 1-1. At 8:41, David Lundbohm skated up the middle 1-on-3 and, with no particular place to go, he flung a long wrist shot past the partial screen of a defender and the puck caught the upper right on Hauser for a 2-1 Sioux lead. After the three goals in a burst of less than three minutes, the game stabilized a little, but with 3:53 left in the first period, Lundbohm scored again, converting a goal-mouth pass for a 3-1 Sioux lead. Next, a skirmish filled the penalty boxes with two players from each side, and moments later another Gopher penalty led to a Sioux power play. While killing that shortage, Jordan Leopold got the puck in his own zone and retreated, trying to use up some seconds before he cleared it. Then he flipped a high, long clearing pass toward the other end, and it happened to be on goal. Everybody in the building, including Kollar, was shocked when the 150-footer hit the ice and skipped right between Kollar's legs with 1:30 remaining to cut the deficit to 3-2.

But just 11 seconds after that, the power play still in effect, Ryan Bayda blew a slapshot in from the top of the right circle and another burst of three goals in a 2:23 span made it 4-2 Sioux at the intermission.

Hauser had given up four goals and made four saves, while Kollar had let in two but made nine saves. Lucia pulled Hauser and sent in freshman Travis Weber. The Sioux crowd loved it, already certain that a blowout victory would be the perfect way to celebrate the opening of the new arena.

In the second period, however, Jeff Taffe struck early for Minnesota, skating to the crease from the right corner and jamming a goal past Kollar to trim the deficit to 4-3. It stayed that way through a couple of power plays, until the midpoint of the period. Matt Jones scored with a partially screened shot from the left point. The puck glanced in off Weber, but it was the only goal he allowed out of 10 shots in that period. It seemed more than enough, however, because the Gophers fired 14 more shots at Kollar before intermission, and he blocked the other 13, securing the rollicking, celebratory mood with a 5-3 lead.

An interesting focal point to the entire Gopher season occurred in the dressing room—the very posh visiting dressing room at Engelstad Arena, where visiting teams can drive their team bus right inside and up to the door. The coaches and the veteran players said things that have been said throughout the history of team sports, things about it "only" being 5-3, and how "C'mon, guys, we can come back from this." That sort of stuff. Most of the players found it to be something resembling lip service. They had heard it before.

"We had spent the whole summer talking about going up there and doing some damage, but the first two periods, it didn't work out that way," said Jordan Leopold. "In seasons past, we never could overcome a deficit in the third period. I don't remember us ever coming from two or three goals behind to win any game."

Nick Angell also could be excused for being a cynic. "We went into that game, and we wanted to get the first goal," he said. "So they got the first, what...three?"

Not quite, but it seemed that way.

"We were down after two periods, and guys are saying we can come back, we can do it," Angell said. "I thought, 'I've been here before.' I don't know how many times I can remember guys saying, 'OK, let's go out and get five goals and win it.'"

The cocaptains made the words spring to life back out on the ice. At 0:27 of the third period, Johnny Pohl squeezed up the right boards and threw a hard pass across the slot. Leopold, always eager and so skilled at moving up to join the offense, drilled it past Kollar, and suddenly it was 5-4. At 2:01, Kollar came sliding out for a big save, but big Jeff Taffe gained possession, circled around from behind the net and stuffed in another goal for a 5-5 deadlock.

The raucous crowd fell into silence, and the Gophers swarmed to attack. At 3:25, a pair of freshmen collaborated when Keith Ballard flipped a shot from the right point and Jon Waibel tipped it past the beleaguered Kollar, putting Minnesota on top at 6-5. At 8:44, Matt Koalska circled to the slot and drilled a 30-footer into the right edge of the net and the Gophers had an improbable 7-5 lead.

Blais pulled Kollar, and the residual effect of that game led to a shaky season for assorted North Dakota goaltenders. Incredibly, while the game turned out to be a major focal point for Minnesota, it worked that way in reverse for the Fighting Sioux, who struggled all season before falling from contention and finishing tied for sixth in the WCHA. Jake Brandt went in and stopped all five shots he faced the rest of the way that night, but the damage had been done. Minnesota outshot North Dakota 14-4 in the third period, and 40-22 for the game, and drove away from the fabulous new Engelstad Arena with a 7-5 victory.

"I don't think anybody thought that two seniors would start and two freshmen would end up in goal in this game," said Minnesota coach Don Lucia right afterward. "There's no explanation for what happened in the first period. I asked Adam, and there are probably a couple of goals he's like to have back. I'm very proud of Travis the way he came in and played. He made some real big saves when it was 5-3.

"There haven't been a lot of third-period comeback wins for us in the last few years."

Indeed, this particular group of Gophers couldn't remember any, on their side.

"I really don't remember much about specific games, when I look back," said Leopold. "That's what Pohl does. He can remember every goal. But I think that North Dakota game was the most important game of the year. There were a lot of other big games, like when we played Colorado College at our place—I think we swept 'em—but the North Dakota game set a scene for us. I can't remember ever coming from that far behind before, but we did it up there. In the third period, we turned on the jets. And when it was over, we looked around at each other and said, 'OK—we can do it this year.'"

Nick Angell tried to fit that game into his context of four-year history. "We started out so bad when I was a freshman, and my second year, we had changed coaches, and the program gradually started coming," Angell said. "Then we made the NCAA regional last year, my third year. This year Bob

Motzko came in as second assistant, and he believed we were good enough to win it all. He came in and said, 'It's our time.' So 'It's our time' became our battle cry.

"At North Dakota, when we won that game 7-5 in their new building, my dad said, 'You guys could win the national championship!' I guess that was the first time I can remember anybody even thinking about that. We'd had so many situations where we were behind during my first three years, when everybody says, 'Let's go get 'em, guys.' But this time, we did it. We played so well and worked so well together, and I think we started building from that first game."

Pohl, the historian as well as prime architect, said: "I think the opening game at North Dakota was one of maybe the three or four most defining games of the season. In my three years, we'd played six games up at Grand Forks. We'd won once, tied once, and that's it—even though we'd have a lead in almost every game. It always seemed to happen that they would come back, get buzzing, then the whole building felt like it was going to collapse, and there's nowhere to run, nowhere to hide.

"So, we go down 4-2 in the first, and Adam wasn't playing well. It was 5-3 going into the third, and I don't think we had come back from two goals down in the third period in years. To do that, up there, what a great way to start the season. There could have been no better way to start the season than to go up there, into North Dakota, get down by two in the third period, and win it. We came back a lot this year. Because of that game, we had confidence until the buzzer sounded that we were going to win—every night, all year."

The Gophers gave North Dakota a 3-1 head start, then rallied for a 7-5 victory in the game that both dedicated Engelstad Arena and Minnesota's championship season.

Chapter 18

Season starts fast
(13 games witout a loss)

IN CASE ANYONE DOUBTS THE POSITIVE IMPACT felt by the Gophers over their third-period reversal for the exhibition victory at North Dakota, just look at what happened in the weeks immediately following that start. The Gophers sailed away, as did Denver and St. Cloud State, and the three promptly established themselves as being among the elite in the country, not just the WCHA.

Each of those games meant different things to different players, but Johnny Pohl was drafted to wade through the games, and their significance.

After the North Dakota game, the Gophers had two weeks off, then had four more non-WCHA encounters, all of which proved to be easy victories.

Bemidji State W7-2, 7-1

Oct. 19-20, Mariucci Arena.

Troy Riddle and Pohl each scored two goals, and Barry Tallackson, Erik Wendell and Jordan Leopold got the others, as the Gophers built a 3-1 lead in the first period of the first game, while Matt Koalska had three assists and Paul Martin and Judd Stevens two apiece in the 7-2 romp. Travis Weber had 20 saves as the Gophers dominated. In the second game, the Gophers won 7-1, with Pohl and Riddle each scoring two goals, and Jeff Taffe, Paul Martin and Pat O'Leary got one each, and Taffe added three assists and Riddle two. Adam Hauser returned to the nets and coasted as the Gophers outshot the Beavers 46-20.

"You don't want to blow one against a team you're supposed to kill," said Pohl. "It was good, but you don't want to choke and blow one. It was nice for our freshmen to get some experience. Adam bounced back in the second game against Bemidji, and Travis got some action."

Colgate W8-0, 9-0

Oct. 26-27 at Mariucci.

"It would have been nice to have these games my second year," said Pohl. "I had five assists the second night against Colgate. But everything we shot went in. Justin got his first game in goal."

Riddle and Nick Anthony got two each in the 8-0 first game as Hauser stopped all 18 shots and Minnesota opened with four goals in the first period. Johnson stopped all 28 for a debut shutout in the second game, as Matt Koalska and Grant Potulny had two goals apiece.

Michigan Tech W7-3, T5-5

Nov. 2-3, Houghton, Mich.

Minnesota spotted the Huskies leads of 1-0 and 2-1 in the first period, and it became 3-1 in the second before the Gophers took charge and scored the next six goals for the 7-3 victory in the first game. Down 3-1 until the 8-minute mark of the second period, the Gophers got close-order goals from Pohl, Paul Martin, and Taffe in a span of 2:23, then Anthony and Wendell scored 9 seconds apart to complete a 5-goal second period. Hauser came back from a rocky start as the Gophers outshot the Huskies 43-27.

"Tech was a place where we probably should sweep, but it's hard to get a sweep in our league," said Pohl. "It probably was good for us. We played well the first night; we were down after one, never panicked, got five in the second. Then we completely laid an egg on Saturday night. We were down 5-1, and we came back, and forced overtime. That was one game that showed how resilient we were, and we got one with the goalie pulled."

In the second game, the Huskies jumped all over Weber, scoring the game's first four goals—two of them by Clay Wilson, a freshman defenseman from Cloquet—on 13 shots before Hauser came on in relief. Potulny's power-play marker cut it to 4-1, but Tech made it 5-1 early in the second. The Gopher comeback started when Riddle scored with both teams shorthanded and freshman Jake Fleming scored his first goal while penalty-killing to trim it to 5-3. Hauser cleared the puck to Leopold, who fed Pohl for a power-play goal midway through the third period, then Pohl set up Leopold for the equalizer with 1:09 left and Hauser pulled for an extra attacker. Hauser stopped 18 of 19 as Minnesota outshot Tech 41-32 to get the tie.

That continued a remarkable trend. Minnesota was 18-1-1 when scoring first, but a very good 14-7-3 when yielding the first goal, as well as 7-4-1 when trailing after one period, and 5-6-2 when behind after two.

Mankato W5-3, 4-2

Nov. 9-10 at Mariucci

The Mavericks see the Gophers as their biggest challenge, which doesn't make them unique—just another "natural" rival for Minnesota.

"They were both tough games, Mankato played us tough," said Pohl. "In the first one it was 1-1 after one, then 2-2 after two, then we got a couple. The second night, we were down 2-0 after one. But we showed we could come back again, and protect a third-period lead. We played well in the third."

The first night, Taffe scored on a 2-man power play, but the Mavericks tied it on a power play of their own. In the second period, Leopold scored unassisted at 0:22, but again Mankato came back to tie on a power play. Pohl's goal on a power play at 15:33 broke the tie and Leopold followed with his second of the game for a 4-2 lead at the intermission. Mankato closed it to 4-3 in the third, but Pohl's power-play goal clinched it. Minnesota outshot Mankato by only 32-27, and Hauser was the winner in goal.

In the second game Mankato led 2-0 on a pair of first-period power plays, but Minnesota came back for goals by Koalska and Leopold in the second period. Keith Ballard scored at 5:46 of the third to break the 2-2 tie, and Taffe hit an empty net with 12 seconds left to clinch it. Justin Johnson stopped 31 of 33 in the Gopher goal, while the Gophers launched 51 shots at freshman Maverick goalie Jon Volp, meaning he faced 83 shots in two nights.

UMD W5-1, 5-3

Nov. 16-17 at Mariucci

As it turned out, the Gophers were able to continue their schedule without any top-five finishers in the first dozen games—a degree of difficulty that would soon change abruptly. However, facing a team like Mankato or UMD is never easy for Minnesota. "If we're playing Duluth, Mankato, or St. Cloud, we know it's going to be a tough game," said Pohl. "Minnesota is never going to blow those teams out. We're their biggest rival, we're the big school and they want to beat us."

Turns out, the first game was easy, on the scoreboard, as the Gophers went up 2-0 in the first period and put the game away with two goals 10 seconds apart midway through the second. But it was tougher than the score showed. UMD was penalized at 0:19, and Potulny tipped in a Taffe shot at 0:43 in the first period. Late in the opening period, Matt DeMarchi shot one off the left goal pipe and the puck landed just beyond the reach of UMD goalie Adam Coole. Defenseman Steve Rodberg reached to gain possession, but Barry

Tallackson arrived at that moment and poke-checked the puck into the net at 16:48 for a 2-0 lead.

Brett Hammond scored a breakaway goal for UMD to open the second period and cut it to 2-1. Midway through the second period, the Gophers proved lightning could strike twice in the same place. Leopold was penalized for holding a stick at 9:08, erasing a Gopher power play. But at 10:05, Nick Angell drilled a screened slapshot from the left point for a shorthanded goal. After the ensuing faceoff, Nick Anthony carried up the left side and scored at 10:15. Two goals in 10 seconds could be devastating; two shorthanded goals on the same penalty kill 10 seconds apart was something beyond devastating. Coole was pulled at that moment, but the damage was done. Johnny Pohl scored the only goal of 18 shots fired at Rob Anderson, connecting midway through the third period, to secure the 5-1 outcome after a 40-21 edge in shots.

The next night, Anderson was brilliant and UMD had a chance to win against Justin Johnson. After Andy Reierson's goal staked UMD to a 1-0 lead, Fleming scored shorthanded and Leopold on a power play for a 2-1 lead at the first intermission. But Judd Medak scored at 0:35 of the second to tie it for UMD, and Jon Francisco scored again, a power-play goal at 3:36. Lucia pulled Johnson, after the only two shots of the period had gone in, and Hauser came off the bench. He stopped all 12 remaining UMD shots, while Minnesota responded with rebound goals by Waibel and Koalska in the second period, and another second-rebound goal, by Wendell, in the third. The 5-3 final wasn't much reward for outshooting the Bulldogs 41-19, but it was sufficient.

"In the 5-1 game, their goalie let in a couple easy ones," said Pohl.. "We came back and had back-to-back shorthanded goals. In the second game, Duluth led 3-2. You know, I'll bet we were trailing over 50 percent of our games this year. After our first five games, we didn't have an easy game till after Christmas."

No, but easy or not the Gophers were off to a 9-0-1 start, excluding the North Dakota opener.

Michigan W5-2, Michigan State T4-4

Nov. 23 at Ann Arbor; Nov. 25 at East Lansing, Mich.

"This was a weekend we proved we could do some big things," said Pohl. "In Ann Arbor, we kind of smoked 'em off the draw. It was 3-0 after the first period, and we were up 5-1 late. They didn't make it 5-2 till the middle of the third."

This time it was Ballard with an unassisted goal, then Jeff Taffe found his goal-scoring touch and scored at 5:06 and 6:51 for a 3-0 lead before the fans were completely seated. The Wolverines scored one midway through the second period, but Taffe completed his hat trick at 14:36 and the Gophers took a 4-1 lead into the third period. DeMarchi's unassisted goal made it 5-1. With no idea that the Wolverines would be a team they would ultimately play in the NCAA semifinals, the Gophers swiped a big game in Ann Arbor despite being outshot 35-32 as Hauser made 33 stops.

"Two days later, playing in East Lansing on Sunday, it was like a heavyweight fight," said Pohl. "Michigan State got the lead, and we came back. They scored three goals in a row. We got the tie when we scored late—Barry Tallackson got the goal with two minutes left."

Michigan State couldn't keep pace with the Gopher forwards, who built a 38-24 edge in shots. After yielding a 1-0 lead, the Gophers responded 25 seconds later when Brett MacKinnon connected, and Potulny scored at 19:45 on a power play. Wendell's 2-man power-play goal made it 3-1 in the second, but Michigan State got one back later in the second period, then added two in the third to regain the lead at 4-3, with three of the four goals against Hauser coming on power plays. That set the stage for Tallackson, whose goal with 2:09 remaining was set up by Pohl.

"It was a great game," said Pohl. "Everyone on our team was beaten up and bruised. We had left everything on the ice."

St. Cloud L2-3, T2-2

Nov. 30 at Mariucci; Dec. 1 at St. Cloud

After a 10-0-2 start, not counting the exhibition victory at North Dakota, the Gophers were on top of the world—at least the college hockey world. But St. Cloud State and Denver also were sizzling and high in national rankings. Having just finished with the CCHA's two top perennial powers in Michigan and Michigan State, Minnesota's schedule didn't get any easier heading back into WCHA play.

When Minnesota and St. Cloud State collided in their usual home-and-home setting, it was the surprising Huskies who took charge, beating Minnesota 3-2 at Mariucci Arena, then blowing a 2-0 lead before settling for a 2-2 tie the next night in St. Cloud.

The first game saw the Huskies jump ahead when freshman Mike Doyle scored a power-play goal, but Leopold tied it for Minnesota on a 2-man edge as Dean Weasler survived a 17-9 Minnesota edge in shots. Defenseman Derek Eastman put St. Cloud back ahead 2-1 in the second period, and Matt Hendricks made it 3-1 on another power play. Barry Tallackson got a power-play goal for Minnesota in the third period, but that was it, as Dean Weasler made 37 saves while Hauser made only 19.

A huge crowd of 10,231 filled Mariucci for that first game, and the next night an overflow 6,685 filled the National Hockey Center in St. Cloud to see a classic duel. The game went scoreless through the first period and 18:18 of the second, when Nate DiCasmirro scored for St. Cloud State. The Huskies got a power play in time to arrange a goal by Jon Cullen seven seconds before the middle period ended, and it was 2-0. Hauser, however, made 17 saves in that second period to hold the Huskies from blowing the game open, and his play—45 saves in all—kept the Gophers in position for a third-period comeback. Tallackson got one goal back at 1:42, and Leopold's power-play goal midway through the period tied it 2-2, which is how it ended, despite Minnesota being outshot 47-27, the most the Gophers were outshot all season.

"They were hot then," said Pohl. "The first night at home we lost, but look at that, we outshot them 39-22 and we lost. You can take one or two things from that. They got a goal, Matt Hendricks completely kicked it in, but the ref couldn't tell. Maybe their other was kicked in, too. We lost, but we definitely felt we were at least as good as they were. Up there the next night, we were down going into the third, but we came back and got two big goals and tied 'em.

"I still don't think anybody was thinking of national title, we were thinking league title then. Then we went out to Denver. They had lost maybe twice all year. We didn't score much."

Denver W2-1, L3-4

Dec. 7-8 in Denver

The first of several showdowns between the two elite powers went to the Gophers, when Paul Martin scored in the first period, Erik Wendell scored in the second, and Hauser held off the Pioneers until freshman Luke Fulghum scored at 12:20 of the third period. Hauser made 30 saves to outduel Denver ace Wade Dubielewicz, as Denver outshot Minnesota 31-23.

The flow of play was more evenly balanced the next night when the Gophers outshot Denver 31-30, but the Gophers had to play from behind all night. Matt Koalska countered an early goal by Max Bull for a 1-1 tie, but Kevin Doell boosted Denver to a 2-1 lead midway through the first period. Aaron MacKenzie scored on an early second-period power play for a 3-1 Denver lead, although Grant Potulny got another for Minnesota midway through the second, and it was 3-2 after two. Chris Paradise got one by Hauser at 1:24 of the third period to recapture the two-goal margin for Denver, and it withstood Riddle's goal for a 4-3 Pioneer victory.

"We played smart, and stayed out of box, in the first game," said Pohl. "The second night, we didn't play well at all. That night, we showed that maybe, deep down, some guys were satisfied with the split, going into the break. Really, just because of the style, they were like a pro team."

Still, 11-2-3 wasn't bad at all, but if the Gophers hinted at the final glory that was to come by going 10-0-1 at the start, they obscured it a bit by tailing off through a 1-2-2 stretch leading into their 20-day Christmas Holiday break.

Adam Hauser left no short-side room for this Maine attempt at a bad-angle goal.

Troy Riddle's exceptional speed allowed him to add a breakaway threat to the first line.

Keith Ballard and Troy Riddle threatened UMD's goal.

Chapter 19

Off-again, on-again

THERE WERE MANY BIG GAMES STILL TO COME, but two of the most significant weekends, in the minds of Johnny Pohl and various other members of the Gopher gang, were the back-to-back series at Minnesota-Duluth and at North Dakota in February. To get there, however, Minnesota came out of Christmas Break and immediately tiptoed into a weird tendency to play poorly one game and very well the other, a true black-and-white, Jekyll-and-Hyde system of contrasting play, with contrasting results.

"We started that little trend where we could not put back to back games together, Friday and Saturday," said Johnny Pohl. "We either played poorly on Friday and great on Saturday, or the opposite."

That strange tendency started slowly, but lasted for eight consecutive weekends, right up until two weeks from the end of the regular season. Friday was the main problem, as the Gophers went 1-5-1 in the first games of a series and 7-0 in the first seven weeks of WCHA play after the year changed to 2002. The weird routine was much more subtle when it first took effect, at the Mariucci Classic, just after Christmas.

Ferris State W3-2, Providence W6-1

Dec. 28-29, 2001 at Mariucci Classic

Ferris State came into Mariucci Arena and gave the Gophers fits in the first game of the Mariucci Classic holiday tournament. It seemed as if the 20-day layoff may have hurt Minnesota, either that or too much Christmas turkey. Nobody was thinking of the Friday Night Blahs at that point.

The teams played a scoreless first period, then Ferris took a 1-0 lead in the second period. Jeff Taffe tied it 1-1 but the Bulldogs went back up 2-1, where it stayed until the third. At that point, freshman Paul Martin looked nothing like a rookie as he scored an unassisted goal to tie the game, and collaborated with Pohl on a power-play set-up to Taffe, whose second goal of the game was the game-winner at 9:11. The Gophers outshot Ferris State 32-27, but needed Adam Hauser to be solid with 13 of his 25 saves in the third period to cling to the 3-2 victory.

"We came back, in the first game, but we did not play well at all," said Pohl. " We were fortunate to come out with the win that night. Ferris is a team we should have beaten much worse. We were up 2-1 going into the third, but Jeff Taffe had a pretty good game. He got a couple goals, but besides him, we didn't play very well at all. We were just fortunate to come out with a win."

In the tournament final, the Gophers got rolling early and never looked back. Barry Tallackson, Erik Wendell and Taffe scored first-period goals in front of Travis Weber, who allowed only a second-period goal. Pohl countered that one almost immediately to make it 4-1 after two periods, and Pohl and Stevens both got their second goals in the third period to romp 6-1, volleying 50 shots at the Friar net compared to the 25 shots Weber faced.

"We came back and just hammered Providence the next night," said Pohl. "They were a pretty good team, but we just took it to them.

"I was with Tallackson and Taffe that night," added Pohl, who had two goals and three assists as that line scored five of the six goals. "That was the weekend he put Taffe on wing instead of center. That only lasted a week or two. We canned that idea."

North Dakota L3-4, W2-1

Jan. 5-6, 2002 at Mariucci Arena

All seemed in order as the Gophers hit the ice and jumped the Fighting Sioux for a 2-0 lead on goals by Troy Riddle at 1:57 and Taffe on a power play late in the first period. The score remained 2-0 through a scoreless second period. But the Fighting Sioux, perhaps still smarting at the recollection of how the Gophers ruined their gala home opener, stalked right back in the third period to return the favor, right in the Gopher home.

First off, that exhibition opener ruined Sioux goaltender Andy Kollar's night, and may have damaged his confidence, because he never seemed to regain his sharpness. He struggled so much that coach Dean Blais went out and recruited a new goaltender at midseason. Josh Siembeda came in from the USHL, and made an impressive debut at Mariucci. After giving up those first two goals he stopped 37 of the remaining 38 shots, holding the Sioux in the game until they could take it over.

Freshmen Brian Canady and James Massen scored in the first 10 minutes to erase the 2-0 Gopher lead, and with 4:16 to go, Ryan Bayda scored to give the Sioux their first lead. The Gophers kept firing, but their 17 shots in the period seemed to lack the required intensity, and when Don Lucia pulled Hauser for an extra attacker, Jason Notermann promptly hit the empty net for a 4-goal turnaround. Potulny's goal with only three seconds to go was too little, and far too late.

"We blew it majorly in the first game," said Pohl. "We were up 2-0 and we played terribly in the third. They just buzzed off and we played terrible. They deserved to win. It was kind of a slap in the face. They were having a tough year, and were kind of bottom of the pack, and we were a pretty good third-period team—until that game. They got an empty-net goal, then we scored with 3 seconds left. They had that new goalie come in, and he played pretty well against us. We had 40 shots the first night and 38 the second."

In the second game, the Gophers bounced back—again displaying their newly established trend of playing poorly one night and very well the other. The Gophers outshot North Dakota 38-22 in the second game, but Siembeda again stymied them most of the way. Travis Weber was in goal, and was dented at 4:35 of the first when freshman defenseman Nick Fuher scored for a 1-0 Sioux lead, and as well as the Gophers were playing, Siembeda was outstanding. Finally, with 7:43 remaining in the third period, and each team a man short, Jordan Leopold scored the equalizer for Minnesota. And with 1:34 left, Leopold scored again and the Gophers got away with a split.

"Jordan bailed us out, big time," recalled Pohl. "We were down 1-0 going into the third and we could not get on the board. Then Leo got two big goals late. He pretty much won that game by himself. Weber played well, with 21 saves out of 22 shots.

"North Dakota having a tough year, but we struggled. We were still thinking we had pretty good shot at league title…. Then we went to Wisconsin the next week and just got hammered."

Wisconsin L3-8, W6-2

Jan. 11-12, 2002 at Madison.

The shiny new Kohl Center had 12,937 fans the first night and 14,711 the second for the Badgers' biggest series of the season. The hockey games were remarkably contrasting, with the Gophers overwhelmingly outshooting Wisconsin in the first game, but getting blown out 8-3, then Minnesota was outshot by the Badgers, but rebounded to hammer the home team.

Adam Hauser had a rocky time of it and played only two periods the first night, when the Badgers scored the first two goals in the first period, before Jon Waibel got one back, then they also scored the first two goals of the second period, including a shorthanded goal by Duluthian Andy Wheeler, and held a 5-2 cushion at the second intermission. The Gophers got a goal each period, by Waibel, Pohl and Taffe, but the Badgers kept rolling, putting three more goals past relief goalie Travis Weber, who made one save.

Strangely enough, the game also meant that the the Gophers lost in a blowout by giving up eight, the most goals they would yield all season, on the same night they recorded 53 shots, their highest shot production of the entire season.

"This was the first of four out of five weekends on the road for us," said Pohl. "The first night, I honestly don't know what happened. We outshot em 53-27. And they were decent shots. It was 19-4 in the third period. It was just one of those nights where we took it to 'em, but they'd come down and put it in the net. They steamrolled us.

"Then the second night was exactly the opposite. They outshot us 36-33, and we stuck it to them. Hauser bounced back and played great, and we scored some power play goals."

In the second game, Matt Hussey duplicated his first-game role of scoring the first goal for the Badgers. But Wisconsin didn't score again on Hauser until the Gophers had rattled six goals into the Badger net. Waibel and Taffe scored 36 seconds apart midway through the first period, while freshman Garrett Smaagaard—who was starting to play late after recovering from football knee surgery that had knocked him out for his entire senior season at Eden Prairie High School—got a goal midway through the second period, and Barry Tallackson made it 4-1 three minutes later.

It kept on rolling in the third period, as Riddle and Leopold scored—Riddle shorthanded and Leo on a power play—for a 6-1 cushion. For the third straight weekend, the Gophers had rebounded from a faltering first game for a dominant rematch.

Alaska-Anchorage T3-3, W5-2

Jan. 8-9 at Anchorage

The off-again, on-again routine persisted after the long flight to Anchorage. The Gophers seemed destined to beat the Seawolves in the first game, which also was the first meeting between coaches Don Lucia and John Hill, who had been Lucia's long-standing assistant at Colorado College and Minnesota before moving home to Anchorage to rebuild the program for the 2001-02 season.

"We played pretty well in that first game, and they scored with one second left and sent it to overtime," said Johnny Pohl. "That was a pretty tough pill to swallow. You hate to have that happen, but that was really tough to see that one point go. It's just weird when you go up to Alaska. You never know what's going to happen."

Barry Tallackson's goal staked Hauser to a 1-0 first-period lead, but the Seawolves tied it 1-1 in the second when freshman John Hopson scored. The Gophers appeared to take charge in the third, when Pohl scored a power-play goal at 0:26 and Grant Potulny scored on another power play at 4:11 for a 3-1 lead. But Dallas Steward closed it to 3-2 with a shorthanded goal at 5:39, and the teams played that way for 14:20 of the remaining 14:21 of regulation. Then, with goaltender Kevin Reiter pulled for a sixth attacker, the always-dangerous Steve Cygan knocked one in from a scramble with one second left. Neither team could score in overtime, and the 3-3 tie stood.

The next night, with Travis Weber in goal, the Gophers fell behind 1-0, but Jeff Taffe tied it at 11:10 of the first period. Troy Riddle scored at 7:40 of the second and assisted Potulny on another at 9:28 for a similar-sounding 3-1 lead after two. Sure enough, Cory Hessler scored for Anchorage at 5:16 of the third to cut it to 3-2, but this time Paul Martin scored with 3:58 left and Taffe scored again into an empty net in the final minute. Pohl assisted on both goals.

"We came back the second night and played much better," said Pohl. "With five minutes left, we were up 3-2, and Paul Martin got one off the draw—my draw, actually. Then Jeff got an empty-net goal. I tipped one off the glass to get it out of the zone, and he whacked one in from center ice."

Denver L1-3, W6-1

Jan. 25-26 at Mariucci

Another critical series against Denver, which ultimately was to win the WCHA with its experienced, often-dominating outfit. Coming off a stretch with no series sweeps in their last five WCHA series, the Gophers were trying to get everything back in order, and after splitting a pair of tight, one-goal games at Denver in early December, the Gophers knew what they were in for. It just didn't seem to matter.

After a scoreless first period, sophomore defenseman Ryan Caldwell put Denver in front 1-0, but Pat O'Leary tied it later in the period. With just 12 seconds to go in the middle period, however, Max Bull scored shorthanded—a pivotal goal that let Denver take a 2-1 lead into intermission. The carryover sent the Pioneers back onto the ice and Greg Keith scored another shorthanded goal at 0:27 of the third period, and goaltender Adam Dubielewicz made the goals stand up with 34 saves.

"We were back at home, in a make-or-break series to get back into the title picture," said Pohl. "We lost the first one, and gave up two shorties, one late in the second and another at the beginning of the third. Their goalie, Wade Dubielewicz, played well, but we outshot 'em 35-21, and we got beat because they got two shorties. When you play a team like that, you can't afford to make mistakes, and we made two crucial mistakes."

Once again, Weber replaced Hauser for the second game in the Gopher net, and he had a comparatively easy night, as the Gophers responded with a 46-23 shot barrage and a 6-1 romp over Denver. Pohl's power-play goal jump-started the Gophers late in the first period, and Erik Wendell and Keith Ballard sandwiched goals around one by Denver's Lukas Dora. Wendell made it 2-1 at 13:01 of the middle period, and after Dora scored on a two-man power play, Ballard connected with 57 seconds left in the session for a 3-1 edge.

Minnesota cruised home in the third period, as Ballard scored again, on a power play, then Taffe scored with 5:47 left on another power play, and Jordan Leopold scored with each side a man short with four minutes left for the 6-1 bulge.

"We came back and played great," said Pohl. "Denver probably had a bad night, but we came out and scored early. It was 3-1 going into third, and we just poured it on. Tallie got a nice goal on power play, Jeff scored on the power play, and Jordan scored. That was nice; we got some confidence back."

But the Gophers were still snagged in a 4-3-1 stretch since the first of the new year, hardly the recipe for a championship, with a finishing run of archrivals UMD and North Dakota, then Colorado College, Wisconsin and St. Cloud State promising no let-up.

Minnesota-Duluth L2-5, W2-1

Feb. 1-2, 2002 at Duluth

"We went up to Duluth and got just killed," said Pohl. "They were in like ninth place, but they had a pretty good finish to their season, and we talked about how well they were playing. Friday night, I'd say it was one of only two or three games all year where we can just say we laid an egg. They wanted it more. The shots were 33-32, but they wanted it way more."

As usual, UMD's only true sellouts were when Minnesota came to town. There were 5,405 at the DECC, but they included a large cluster of Gopher fans who somehow wound up seated in the lower level, right behind the UMD goaltender, in easy heckling range, for two periods out of three each night. Interestingly, Lucia chose to play freshman Travis Weber in goal instead of Adam Hauser.

The pace was intense, with UMD's Andy Reierson scoring from the right point at 2:42, and Jeff Taffe countering by skating in to retrieve a loose puck and fire a screened wrist shot from the top of the right circle at 13:35. But the Bulldogs pulled off their biggest period of the season, or several seasons, when they scored four unanswered goals in the second period. Freshman Evan Schwabe beat Weber on a power-play wraparound at 1:14. Senior Judd Medak blasted right through Weber, taking the puck into the net with him for a 3-1 lead at 7:37. Two minutes later, senior Tom Nelson scored on a rebound scramble for a 4-1 lead, and Lucia yanked Weber and sent in Hauser.

Nelson scored again on a power play at 13:13, and UMD led 5-1. A goal by Jordan Leopold later in the second period didn't help much. Some frustration seemed evident when Jon Waibel ran into UMD goaltender Rob Anderson in the crease, which led to a major scrap that assured the penalty boxes would be busy into the third period.

"Even up 5-1, no lead feels comfortable against those guys," said UMD coach Scott Sandelin. "I was ready for them to come out in the third period and—look out! But they've been playing better on Saturday night, and we've played bettrer on Saturday too."

Lucia was matter-of-fact. "We got out-goaltended, out-special-teamed and they deserved to win the game," said Lucia. "It seems that on Fridays we back off a little, then on Saturdays we play harder because we think it's more important. We had a chance to finish our checks and we skated by people. We were playing against a team that played harder, but that's part of our growing process. We got outworked—really outworked—but we've got a lot of road games, and it's got to come from within."

Two months later, Leopold still remembered that game. "Everybody is looking to beat you," said Leopold. "If we play subpar, or even a par game, everybody plays their best. Like UMD or something, our guys think, 'They won't be great.' Then look what happens."

What happened was that the first-game loss at Duluth was something of a watershed for the Gophers. At that point, Minnesota's record of 10-6-3 in the WCHA was still solid. On the other hand, a team that had opened the season 10-0-1 overall, deserving of the No. 1 rank in the country with a pair of five-game winning streaks separated by only one tie, had more impressively also started 5-0-1 in the WCHA. But the Gophers then started to misfire. When they lost that 5-2 game to UMD, the Gophers had recorded a 5-6-2 WCHA stretch that effectively had allowed Denver and St. Cloud State to pull away up ahead.

At the time, however, the Gophers weren't thinking about the big picture so much as getting out of the DECC without losing again.

In the rematch, Minnesota outshot UMD in every period of the Saturday game for a 44-33 edge, but Hauser met his match against UMD sophomore Adam Coole, who not only played up to the standard Rob Anderson had shown in the first game, but was brilliant on his own. He stopped all 17 shots in the first period, and all 15 Gopher shots in the second, and 42 shots in all, while Jon Francisco staked the home club to a 1-0 lead. That put UMD—a team trying to escape last place—in position to sweep a Gopher team that was shooting for the WCHA title.

UMD had to face Minnesota's dazzling power play three times in the third period, including one carryover penalty from late in the second. Another Gopher power play midway through the third period was stalled off, but only seconds later, Jordan Leopold's shot from center point was tipped down and on goal by John Pohl, but was blocked by Coole. But Pohl reached over the fallen goaltender to poke in the rebound at 9:21 for a 1-1 tie. At 10:45, UMD's Reierson was called for hooking, the third straight penalty on the Bulldogs, and a call that drew hostile response from the crowd of 5,405.

UMD had somehow defused the Gopher power play on all 10 of its weekend chances—until then. Six seconds later, a familiar scenario unfolded. Johnny Pohl won a right-corner faceoff and got the puck back to the point, where Leopold fired, and Jeff Taffe knocked in his 24th goal of the season. Hauser held on, and the Gophers escaped from the DECC with a 2-1 victory.

Right after the game, Pohl said: "Five on five, they killed us. We're lucky to come out of here with a split."

Also right after the game, Coach Lucia said: "When Taffe hit a pipe for the second time in the game, I thought maybe it just wasn't our night. If we ended up losing, I could have lived with it, because Coole was great."

After the season, however, looking back on that series, Pohl suggested the reversal of that second game might have been more significant than it seemed at the time. One of the problems with a "lose-on-Friday/win-on-Saturday" tendency is that after losing the first game, there are no guarantees of winning the second game.

"That second night, we were down 1-0, and if we got swept in Duluth, it would have really dampened a lot of spirits," said Pohl. "Especially going up to North Dakota the next week. I remember I scored on a rebound halfway through the third period, then they got a penalty, and two minutes later, Jeff scored. They pulled their goalie with like a minute and a half left, but they didn't come close to even getting in the zone."

The victory also allowed Minnesota to improve that record to 6-6-2 since the 5-0-1 WCHA start. But nobody could have guessed the victory also would start a finishing surge of 11-0-1 through the rest of the regular season and into the WCHA playoff final.

North Dakota W6-4, W4-3

Feb. 8-9, 2002 at Grand Forks

The return trip to Ralph Engelstad Arena signalled an end to Minnesota's routine of shaky first games and much sharper second games. Trouble was, it also seemed to just transfer to a strong first game and a shakier second game. The Fighting Sioux, though, had faltered from their midseason challenge. The strong debut by goaltender Josh Siembada also had come back down to earth, and Coach Dean Blais used Roseau's Jake Brandt, another freshman, in goal both nights.

"The first night, we had a great second period," said Johnny Pohl. "We were up 4-1 at one point, they made it 4-2, we made it 5-2. They pulled their goalie and got two goals with their goalie pulled. And then, the crowd made it crazy in there. We took another penalty in the last minute, and we were ahead by one. With the open net, I just shot the puck from our own faceoff dot and it curved and went in, and we got out of there 6-4."

Pat O'Leary had given the Gophers a 1-0 lead in the opening minutes, but Jason Notermann tied it with 26 seconds left in the first period. Jeff Taffe, Barry Tallackson and Dan Welch scored for Minnesota in the second period. When Tallackson got his second goal, at 8:07 of the third period, it was 5-2. But, as Pohl said, things got a little dicey after that. Freshman Justin Johnson was in goal for Minnesota, and had played well until Tim Skarperud and Aaron Schneekloth scored in a three and a half minute burst to leave it up to an empty-net finish.

There were 11,815 at Engelstad for the first game, and the same figure appeared the next night when the Gophers seemed to figure that they didn't have a bad night Friday, so they could afford a little dip on Saturday. Goaltender Adam Hauser said he was somewhat surprised when he didn't get the call for the second game, but freshman Johnson went back into the nets. David Lundbohm scored at 6:20 of the first period and Andy Schneider made it 2-0 for the Sioux at 8:00, and while Minnesota got untracked when Jake Fleming scored late in the first period, Ryan Hale opened the second period with a goal at 0:24. Down 3-1, Lucia pulled Johnson and sent Hauser in for relief.

Hauser insisted he did nothing more than stop some shots he found routine, and was actually annoyed that his teammates acted as though he had played spectacularly by stopping the last 18 North Dakota shots through the second and third periods. But it provided the springboard for the Gophers to come back.

Johnny Pohl scored a power-play goal at 9:02 of the third, and Pohl scored again, with 3:12 remaining, to tie it 3-3. Jon Waibel scored the winner, with 10 seconds left.

"The second game was very similar to the first game we played up there," Pohl said. "We did not come ready to play—at all. They were up 2-0 in the first and we got it to 2-1. We didn't do anything in the second and they got it to 3-1. I can't remember if something was said in the locker room or what, but we came back. I got two, to make it 3-3. Then Jon Waibel got the biggest goal of his career. It was nice, on a great play by Troy Riddle, and Jon Waibel backhands it in with 10 seconds to go, and we win.

"I think they were shocked by that. Like, I think they were surprised that we came back the first time, in the exhibition game. But the way we won that time, 4-3, I think it stunned them. It even surprised us a little bit.

"The thing I remember about that one, if you came back to the locker room, you'd have thought we had just won the Stanley Cup. We were celebrating, throwing water, and everybody was riding high."

Understandably, because the sweep proved to all the players that while they would win when they played their game, they also could find a way to win when they were *off* their game. That restored the kind of confidence they once had, but had misplaced for about three months.

"Those three games—coming back to beat Duluth in the second game, and the two games at North Dakota—were defining games for us."

Travis Weber was surprised when UMD's Judd Medak hurtled over him, and took the puck into the net as well.

Chapter 20

Gophers finish regular season

THE BIGGEST FACTOR, statistically, in Minnesota's comeback for the second-game 2-1 victory at Duluth was that it ended a struggle that ultimately cost the Gophers a shot at winning the WCHA regular-season title. The sweep at North Dakota the following weekend started a mini-winning streak of three games, but that was far better than never winning two in a row in league play since before Thanksgiving—November 16-17 when UMD came to Mariucci, to be specific. The only time the Gophers had won two in a row since then was when they managed to get past Ferris State and Providence in their own Mariucci Classic over Christmas break, but even that was flanked by WCHA losses on both sides.

If 2002 was supposed to start with Happy New Year, Minnesota started it by going only 4-4-1, so coming out of that funk with the three-game win streak was a definite plus. However, it was time for another rude lesson.

Colorado College L5-6, W7-3

Feb. 15-16, 2002 at Mariucci Arena

Their on-again, off-again play through the second half of the season had dropped the Gophers off the sizzling pace of Denver and St. Cloud State, and, don't look now, but here comes Colorado College. Typical of a Scott Owens-coached team, the Tigers didn't sprint to the top when the season started, but there was no question they had improved into a solid team that skated into contention down the stretch. The CC Tigers came into Mariucci Arena, and both teams had a ton on the line.

"Here we come again," sighed Johnny Pohl. "We're beating them 4-3 in the third the first game, and we totally laid an egg. They came out and scored two, quickly, then another one, so they were up 6-4. We still had eight minutes left, but that was it. That one really hurt. We should have had all the motivation, because we were right even with them, so if we swept them, it would really be important. But we didn't, and we lost."

Minnesota outshot Colorado College 48-30 in the game, but this was another one of those games that made Hauser a bit skeptical of Coach Lucia's claim that his goaltending decisions were all part of a master plan. Freshman Travis Weber started, and fellow-freshman Justin Johnson relieve him, while Hauser was kept in reserve. Meanwhile, Jeff Sanger was certain to give CC spectacular goaltending, both nights. He didn't disappoint, making 43 saves.

Chris Hartsburg staked CC to a 2-0 lead by scoring two goals in the first period. Nick Anthony got Minnesota untracked with a goal at 1:03 of the second, and when Matt DeMarchi scored at 3:54, it appeared the Gophers had recovered sufficiently. Instead, Mark Cullen put CC up 3-2, but Pohl scored with 3:11 to go in the middle period and Dan Welch scored with 1:04 left to vault Minnesota to a 4-3 lead with a period to go and 10,219 home fans urging a victory.

But, just as Pohl recalled, the lights went out when Jason Josza scored for CC at 3:16, and Alex Kim scored at 4:49. The two goals in less than two minutes boosted the Tigers to a 5-4 lead, and when Noah Clarke scored at 9:39, making it 6-4, Lucia pulled Weber, who had made 24 saves but allowed six goals. Johnson went in and played the final 10:29, and was not credited with facing a single shot as the Gophers rallied. Anthony scored his second goal of the game with 7:40 remaining, but Sanger slammed the door and the Tigers won 6-5.

The next night, Hauser was back in goal but the Gophers still had to come back, after Colin Stuart's goal gave CC a 1-0 lead in the first period. Paul Martin, Anthony, and Nick Angell scored in succession to lift Minnesota to a 3-1 lead in the second period. But the Tigers battled back for goals by Clarke and Kim, less than two minutes apart, and CC was even at 3-3. The third period showed the Gophers at full force, however, as Riddle came flying out to score at 0:17 with both teams short a man, and Jordan Leopold scored with Pohl and Riddle assisting at 1:30 to boost Minnesota into the lead at 5-3. Grant Potulny scored on a power play four minutes later and Erik Wendell put one away late in the period for the 7-3 final.

"In the second game, it was 3-3 going into the third," said Pohl. "Then we had a great third period. It turned out to be a really good night. We got four goals and won 7-3.

"It was another of those weekends where we proved we could beat anybody, but we also proved anybody could beat us."

The series did signal the end to the weird Friday/Saturday turnabouts, which had haunted the Gophers for two full months. As mysteriously as it started, and continued to haunt the team for two full months, it just seemed to fade away.

Wisconsin W6-3, W4-3 OT

Feb. 22-23, 2002 Mariucci Arena

Having swept 8-3 and 6-2 romps against the Badgers in Madison six weeks earlier, the return series in Mariucci Arena may not have figured to be that tough. But, again, any Minnesota-Wisconsin series renders form charts meaningless.

"This would be the last time the seniors would play Wisconsin," said John Pohl. "We came in, and smoked 'em. We were up 5-2 in the second period, and made it 6-2 before they got the last goal."

Pohl, of course, figured into the scoring, setting up Jeff Taffe for the first-period power play that clicked at 17:24 to break the scoreless tie. Tight as the score was, Minnesota outshot Wisconsin 21-10 in the opening period, before easing off to a 46-29 edge in the game. But Andy Wheeler tied the game for the Badgers early in the second period, and it stayed 1-1 until 7:14 of the second. Then the Gophers erupted. Pohl scored to break the tie, Taffe scored shorthanded a couple of mintes later, then Dan Welch and Matt DeMarchi scored 20 seconds apart and Minnesota had wrested a 5-1 lead.

Wheeler, who also set up Rob Vega for Wisconsin's second goal at the end of the second period, scored his second of the night in the third period, but not before Nick Anthony had scored at 0:27 to make it 6-2.

The Badgers lifted their level of play in the rematch, outshooting Minnesota 34-32, and they held an early lead on Erik Jensen's goal before Pohl's power-play goal made it 1-1. Pohl scored his second and Taffe got one for a 3-1 lead that seemed to put things in Minnesota's hands in the second period, but Wisconsin came back. Before the middle period ended, freshman Alex Leavitt scored with 2:20 to go and Matt Doman got one past Adam Hauser with 1:30 left, and the Badgers had knotted the game 3-3.

Nobody scored in the third period, but Jordan Leopold came through in overtime, scoring the game-winner at 2:01.

"In the second game, they outshot us and probably deserved to win," said Pohl. "But Jordan bailed us out, scored a big goal. Jordan made a nice move in overtime, and we won. Adam Hauser was playing every night by then."

Leopold also remembers that victory over Wisconsin as being the game that got the Gophers to move beyond the after-effects of their midseason blahs.

"We were having a lot of struggles until we had that overtime win against Wisconsin," Leopold said. "I scored the game-winner. Johnny and I have talked about that. That was at Mariucci. We swept, and it was our first sweep at home since New Year's. We had a funk going on. It wasn't anything we could figure out. Everybody wants to kick your ass. We just needed to finally win one, then we got it."

Saint Cloud State W5-4, W3-1

March 1 at Saint Cloud, March 2 at Mariucci

Saint Cloud State was still in the thick of the race for the WCHA title, but the edge had been taken off just a bit and it was the Huskies who were struggling. The series against Minnesota was obviously their biggest of the season. But Minnesota was unwilling.

An early power play led to a goal by front-of-the-net specialist Grant Potulny at 1:50, and Troy Riddle made it 2-0 at 6:22. Mark Hartigan, St. Cloud's Hobey Baker finalist, scored against Adam Hauser at 15:17 on a power play, but Barry Tallackson made it 3-1 for the Gophers at the first intermission. Taffe opened the second period with a power-play goal at 0:19, and at 1:51, big Nick Angell blasted in a power-play shot from the point and it was 5-1.

To the Huskies credit, they responded for a power-play goal by Jon Cullen before the second period ended, then got goals from Matt Hendricks and Hartigan in the first seven minutes of the third period, challenging the rest of the way but unable to get the equalizer against Hauser.

"Up there, we had a huge lead," said Johnny Pohl. "We were up 5-2 going into the third and we kind of laid an egg again. With 13 minutes to go, they had come back to make it a 1-goal game. We got out huge early, then they came back. When it was 5-4, we shut it down. They didn't get many chances after that. We bent but didn't break that night. It was close to breaking, but it didn't."

Returning to Mariucci Arena the next night, the game seemed to lack the usual crackling intensity the series has become known for. Maybe the Huskies were flat from the previous night, but nobody scored in the first period, and Minnesota went up 2-0 when Matt Koalska and Paul Martin scored in a 1:35 span in the first four minutes of the second period. The Gophers then seemed to put it on cruise control, and Adam Hauser blanked the Huskies until after

Pohl scored unassisted at 0:27 of the third period for a 3-0 cushion. Ryan Malone scored on a 5-on-3 power play at 2:25, but that was the only puck to elude Hauser, as St. Cloud State outshot the Gophers 26-23.

"We just kind of had a ho-hum game," said Pohl. "But we outplayed them. There was a low number of shots on goal, they had 26 we had 23. It was kind of a boring game. I scored, when my shot hit their defenseman and I picked up the puck and backhanded it in. We were up 3-0, They came back and got a 5-on-3 goal. But not much happened after that. We were better than they were at that point in the year. They were just like us the year before. They were struggling right then, and never got it back the whole rest of the season, a lot like we were the year before."

The sweep was enormous for Minnesota, even though the Gophers didn't think they played all that well. It was important for them to establish the routine of winning again, and maybe especially winning when they were struggling, as a lesson for the upcoming playoffs. In the playoffs, they played well, but a lot of that might have been inspiration from remembering how much tougher it was to win when they weren't on their game.

Also, it gave the Golden Gophers a 28-7-4 regular-season record, the best winning percentage since the 1987-88 league title team. A subtle point, however, was that the Gophers had emerged from that 5-6-2 swoon against league foes to finish with an almost-overlooked five-game winning streak, and had also won eight of nine games. The perfect tonic for rising toward a peak for the playoffs—although that peak was still way off, and obscured by a lot of clouds.

Johnny Pohl (9), Jordan Leopold (9) and Matt DeMarchi (19) shared Adam Hauser's pain after a UMD goal in a 5-2 loss – the last Gopher loss before Minnesota's 11-1 surge through the homestretch.

Matt DeMarchi (19) appeared to be unscrewing a Bulldog's head while allegedly trying to help break up a fracas at the UMD goal.

Chapter 21
WCHA playoffs

No matter how the season came out, the Gophers, who had moved back to the level of being a WCHA contender during the 2001-02 season, still had the utmost respect for North Dakota, a program that slid to a tie for sixth place. After all, the Sioux had won three of the previous four league titles while taking second the other year, and won two NCAA titles in the previous five years.

So, even though the Gophers had opened the season by ruining the celebration of the new North Dakota arena, and even though they had beaten the Fighting Sioux in four out of five meetings overall this season, the Minnesota players were less than thrilled about drawing North Dakota as their first-round WCHA playoff opponent.

First Round

North Dakota W7-2, W4-3

"We got third seed, and we go to North Dakota. I don't know how that works," said Johnny Pohl.

The first of a best-of-three series at Mariucci Arena proved the Gopher apprehensions were unnecessary, as the Gophers steamrolled their way to a 7-2 romp. Pohl had two goals and two assists in the first two periods, as the Gophers jumped ahead 2-0 in the first period and 6-1 after two. The line of Pohl with Nick Anthony and Troy Riddle on the wings scored both first-period goals and the first one in the second period,

"The first game was unbelievable," said Pohl. "We were just on fire. We had an edge of 46-23 in shots, and it ended 7-2. It was 6-0 halfway through the game. In the third period, Jordan and I didn't even play. They said we should get rested up. Everything went wrong for North Dakota and right for us. I think we were a little scared. North Dakota had played in the national title game the year before. Whenever we respected an opponent, maybe a little scared, we played well."

Pohl scored early, at 2:17, and Riddle connected at 4:57, and Anthony made it 3-0 just 17 seconds into the second period. At that point, with each member of the line scoring a goal, they also each had two assists. Barry Tallackson scored at 2:59, and Pohl scored on a power play for a 5-0 bulge at 4:02. Two minutes later, Keith Ballard's tally gave Minnesota a 6-0 cushion and only 6:08 of the second period had been reached. Tim Skarperud finally broke through Adam Hauser's shutout bid at 11:28 of the second, but Taffe made it 7-1 in the third before the Sioux got a shorthanded goal to close out the romp. Minnesota outshot the Sioux 46-23.

With 10,203 in the expanded Mariucci Arena both nights, the Gophers ended the series in Game 2, but not without a struggle. Freshman Rory McMahon, who had scored the shorthanded goal at the end of the first game, scored to give the Sioux a 1-0 lead with another shorthanded goal after only 1:10 of the first period. Minnesota bounced back for goals by Dan Welch and Jordan Leopold in the second, but Ryan Bayda tied it 2-2 with 14 seconds left in the middle period.

Taffe's goal at 7:21 of the third boosted Minnesota to a 3-2 edge, but Chad Mazurak tied it again, with 1:07 remaining in regulation, forcing overtime. Keith Ballard scored at 18:36 of overtime, and the Gophers eliminated the Sioux, with the Gophers outshooting North Dakota 52-33, and Hauser making 30 saves to 48 stops for Andy Kollar.

"The second night we didn't play well at all," said Pohl. "Adam played pretty well. They scored with a minute to go in the game, and their goalie pulled, to tie it. It was a long overtime, 18 minutes, when Ballard scored. It was huge for us. If we had lost, I don't know what would have happened to us. My god, if they had beaten us, I don't know if we would have made the NCAAs."

Chapter 22

WCHA Final Five

MINNESOTA AND DENVER SKATED into the WCHA playoff championship game with victories on a big day for homestate hockey at the Xcel Energy Center, where a state record college hockey crowd of 18,523 watched the Gophers whip St. Cloud State 4-1 in the second semifinal.

Semifinals: March 15, 2002 Xcel Energy Center, St. Paul

St. Cloud State W4-1

The Gophers (29-7-4) worked steadily and hard to pull ahead of the archrival Huskies, while goaltender Adam Hauser blanked St. Cloud State until the middle of the third period, when the Gophers already had four goals on the board. Homestaters Jordan Leopold, Troy Riddle, Jeff Taffe and Matt Koalska got the Minnesota goals, while Johnny Pohl set up two of them and Riddle added two assists to his goal.

In the afternoon semifinal, Denver University (31-7-1) beat Colorado College 3-0 in quite similar fashion, scoring a goal in each period—two of them by Twin Cities native Chris Paradise—then entrusting the lead to all-WCHA goaltender Wade Dubielewicz, who stopped all 26 CC shots.

St. Cloud State (29-9-2) and Colorado College (25-12-3) were thus relegated to the third-place game, which could become important for NCAA seeding, because all four semifinalists are expected to be named to the 12-team NCAA tournament field.

The Gophers struck just 55 seconds into the first period, when Pohl fed Riddle for a hard shot from right wing. St. Cloud State goaltender Jake Moreland kicked out his right leg and got a toe on the shot, but the rebound bounced straight out the slot, and Leopold was first to it, slamming a shot that glanced past Moreland.

The goal was the 20th of the season for all-WCHA and All-America defenseman Leopold, breaking the school record for single-season goals by a defenseman.

The teams traded penalties the rest of the first period, and on through the action-filled second period. But 17 seconds before the middle period ended, the Gophers took some of the steam out of the Huskies when Pohl caught a pass as he broke toward the net, only to curl to his right to gain full attention of the defense before sending a neat little back pass to Riddle, who got off an explosive slapshot that beat Moreland and caught the extreme left edge of the net.

The 2-0 lead looked good, and it looked better 35 seconds into the third period, when Jeff Taffe cut right-to-left across the slot, and drilled a hard wrist shot just past a screening body and into the upper right extremity of the net for a 3-0 cushion.

At 7:03, Matt Koalska backhanded a rebound in for a power-play goal and a 4-0 Gopher lead. St. Cloud State coach Craig Dahl replaced Moreland with Dean Weasler for the last 10 minutes, and while that had no effect on the offense, the Huskies did retaliate for a goal at 11:32, when Ryan Malone moved in unmolested from the right corner and forced a shot through Hauser on a power play to make it 4-1.

Denver's victory was remarkably similar. Paradise, who grew up 10 miles north of Xcel Center in Shoreview, scored midway through the first period to stake the Pioneers to a 1-0 lead, which could have been worse but for the sterling play of CC goaltender Jeff Sanger, who also played in Thursday night's overtime victory over Wisconsin to qualify for the semifinals.

Greg Keith made it 2-0 at 14:10 of the second period, capitalizing when a careless back-pass in the neutral zone slid between the two Tiger defensemen, and Keith got to it first for a breakaway. Paradise came through again at 12:10 of the third period with the play of the game. Rushing end to end up the left boards, Paradise put on a late burst of speed, then turned the corner and powered past the last defenseman, veering in front of the net, from where he flicked a late shot up into the short side.

"I thought we played methodically to come out and win each period 1-0," said Denver coach George Gwozdecky, the league's coach of the year. "We've had three goals from the start of the season, and winning the regular season was not even one of them. First was winning the WCHA playoff championship, second was qualifying for a first-round bye in the NCAA, and third was winning the national championship.

"Chris Paradise has been looking forward to coming back here to play in front of his family and friends. He has tremendous skills, he's big, strong, and his two goals—especially the second one—are typical of what he can do."

Paradise said: "The only time I was ever in Xcel Center was when I was home at Christmas and went to a Wild game. It's always been a dream of mine to play in the WCHA, and another dream is to come home and have a chance to win the WCHA championship here."

However, if Denver is the league's best regular-season team, they had to get by the Gophers—the league's hottest team.

Pohl reflection

"We completely outplayed St. Cloud," said John Pohl. "From the drop of the puck, we were more ready. Just like 100 percent opposite of the year before. We were up 4-0, they scored a power play late. They scored with about five minutes left. One of those things.

"I attribute the way we played to the end of our season as juniors, when they swept us and killed us both nights at the end of the year, and absolutely killed us in the Final Five. This was an absolute reversal. Yeah, that motivated us. And we had some confidence because of the way we played 'em in the series at the end of the regular season."

Championship

Denver L2-5

As cool, poised and methodical as a pro team, Denver University scored in all three periods and beat Minnesota 5-2 in the championship game of the WCHA Final Five tournament, before 18,126 fans at Xcel Energy Center. It was the first time since North Dakota in 1997 that the same team had won the MacNaughton Cup for the regular-season WCHA title and the Broadmoor Trophy as playoff champ.

The big crowd ran the five-game tournament total to 75,151, eclipsing the year-old record set last year, the first in the Xcel Center. Adjusted tournament crowds for suite sales were 13,103 Thursday night, 12,438 Friday afternoon, 18,523 Friday night, and 12,961 Saturday afternoon, before the final 18,126.

The Gophers played hard from start to finish, but had their winning streak stopped at nine straight by the brilliant goaltending of Wade Dubielewicz, who made 38 saves, as if he needed to reinforce his stature as the league's top goalie by adding the tournament most valuable player award.

The Pioneers were pro-like in their error-free attention to detail in their own zone. David Neale scored in the first period, Kevin Ulanski and Max Bull in the second, and, after the Gophers closed it to 3-2 by the second intermission, the Pioneers finished it when Greg Barber scored on a breakaway at 8:11 of the third period. Barber punctured Minnesota's final hopes by flipping a long clearing pass up the left boards, and Kevin Doell raced to it and backhanded the puck into an empty net from an extremely wide angle with 45 seconds remaining.

Denver (32-7-1) and Minnesota (29-8-4) are both certain to advance to the NCAA tournament, and they are expected to be joined by Colorado College and St. Cloud State as well.

Colorado College (26-12-3) finished a gruelling three games in less than three days stretch by beating St. Cloud State 2-1 in the third-place game, as Jeff Sanger, the goaltender who beat Wisconsin in overtime Thursday and lost 3-0 to Denver in Friday's semifinals, came back to stop 35 of 36 shots. St. Cloud State is 29-10-2. The Huskies lost twice in two days at the Final Five, a tournament they won last year. This year, that was left to the Gophers and Denver to decide.

Denver struck for a 1-0 lead in the first period on a goal by Neale at 3:32. The Pioneers had an early power play when Erik Wendell was called for hooking Greg Keith into a breakaway spill that resulted in a head-first tumble into the goal post at 2:25. Ryan Caldwell carried deep on the right and passed to the slot where Neale only got a piece of his shot, but enough to send it sliding under the armpit of the sprawling Adam Hauser.

The Pioneers made it 2-0 when Jesse Cook fired from the right point at 1:29 of the second period and the puck hit Kevin Ulanski, who was jostling for position in front of the net when the puck hit him and glanced in.

Minnesota cut it to 2-1 on a controversial goal that had to withstand a video review exactly one minute later. Matt Koalska rushed up the left and passed hard across the slot, but the puck hit Barry Tallackson's skate and caromed back to defenseman Keith Ballard, who quickly shot it into the left edge, past goaltender Wade Dubielewicz—the first goal he had allowed in two tournament games.

Referee Tom Goddard was summoned to stop the game and pause while the goal was reviewed. The replay showed that just before the goal, Wendell had skated directly into the crease and kicked Dubliewicz's left leg. The goalie was understandably knocked to his left, just as the shot flew past him on his right. While officials in this tournament have whistled play dead and faced off outside the zone for merely skating through the crease, this time they decided to allow the goal and it was 2-1.

Undaunted, Denver came back to make it 3-1 at 4:03 when a forechecker knocked the puck free from Jeff Taffe in the Gopher zone, and Max Bull moved in to drill a slapshot into the left edge of the goal.

The Gophers got a key goal back at 13:38 of the middle period, when former Duluth East star Nick Angell cranked a power-play shot from the left point, wide to the left, where Riddle was able to deflect it past Dubliewicz and make it 3-2.

But when the Gophers pressed in the third period, the Pioneers sprung Greg Barber for a breakaway, and Barber rushed up the left side, cutting to the net unmolested and firing a shot that hit Hauser's legpad and carried in at 8:11.

The game took an odd turn after that. Hauser, possibly frustrated, was called for slashing at 11:13, and Grant Potulny served the sentence. At 12:48, Hauser stepped out, grabbed and body-slammed Denver's Greg Keith and was called for holding, this time with Dan Welch serving for him. That left the Gophers in need of a rally, but instead killing a two-man disadvantage—both via penalties on the goalkeeper.

CC Upends Huskies 2-1

Colorado College, hoping to secure its position in the NCAA field, battled St. Cloud State as well as exhaustion and came up winning both matches. Not that it was easy. The Huskies, trying to get things together after a faltering finish, outshot the Tigers 36-25 and took the early 1-0 lead on a goal by Colin Peters.

But after Peters scored at 5:02, goaltender Jeff Sanger simply slammed the door on the Huskies, who still stumbled into the NCAA tournament after having gone 3-5 in their last eight games. The Tigers tied it on a screened shot from center point by Richard Petiot at 6:39 of the first period, and the go-ahead goal came at 3:48 of the second, when Chris Hartsburg scored a power play goal on a rush to the slot.

After that, it was all goaltending, and while Dean Weasler played well for St. Cloud, Sanger was flawless the rest of the way for CC.

"Jeff Sanger gave us three outstanding games in less than three days," said CC coach Scott Owens.

Hartsburg chose to talk more about his goaltender than his goal, as well. "I just want to say that Jeff Sanger is the reason we're here. He made five unbelievable saves in the third period," said Hartsburg. "Jeff has put us in position to go into the NCAA and maybe make some noise there."

Sanger said as a senior, he recalls vividly when Colorado College lost to Michigan State in the final minutes of the NCAA regional at Madison, preventing the Tigers from going to the final four. The next year, the Tigers were upset and didn't even reach the WCHA Final Five. "As seniors, we realize how close we were to making it, and we try to instill the feeling to the freshmen that when you get a chance, make the most of it because you don't know when you'll get another chance."

All-Tournament

The all-WCHA-tournament team included Denver's goaltender Wade Dubielewicz, who also was most valuable player, plus Chris Paradise at a forward slot and defenseman Ryan Caldwell, and Gophers Jordan Leopold on defense and Troy Riddle at forward. The other forward was Colorado College center Mark Cullen.

Jordan Leopold chased behind the net as Adam Hauser kept a wary eye on the St. Cloud Huskies in the WCHA Final Five semifinals.

Adam Hauser sprawled under heavy pressure at the Minnesota goal, as Denver beat the Gophers for the WCHA playoff championship – the only loss in the Gophers' last 12 games, and one that the players say caused them to refocus on the NCAA tournament.

Gopher goalie Adam Hauser proved the old adage about being both good and lucky as he turned acrobat to survive one St. Cloud attack while Jordan Leopold (3) and Matt DeMarchi (19) defended (above), then he got lucky when a rebound squirted through but Ryan Malone was unable to knock it into the open net (below) as Keith Ballard tried to help.

Chapter 23

Lucia's regional plan

EVEN THOUGH WE WERE PLAYING for the WCHA playoff championship, our goal was to get to NCAA," said Minnesota Coach Don Lucia. "We achieved that."

Yes, when Minnesota was beaten, decisively, in the 5-2 WCHA playoff final by Denver, Lucia announced his own perspective, which sounded a lot like a chapter out of the coach's handbook for positive reinforcement, to be deployed as a springboard after any loss that isn't the end of the world—or at least the season.

With the Gophers standing so strong in overall record and strength of schedule, it was a certainty they would be invited to the 12-team NCAA post-season party. And they were. In the West Regional at Ann Arbor, Denver was the No. 1 seed and Minnesota No. 2, meaning those two would get first-round byes. Michigan State (No. 3) would face Colorado College (No. 6), and Michigan (No. 4) would take on St. Cloud State (No. 5). In the East Regional, at Worcester, Mass., New Hampshire was No. 1 and Boston University No. 2, with byes, awaiting first-round games between Maine (No. 3) against Harvard (No. 6), and Cornell (No. 4) against Quinnipiac (No. 5).

Nobody could have guessed that the selection committee would decide, for the first time under the current format, to assign all the west teams in the West Regional at Ann Arbor, and send all the eastern teams to the East Regional in Worcester. When the 12-team, two regional format originated, the plan called for the top four of six teams from each division to stay at home, while the bottom two in each were swapped to the other bracket for crossover games, the perfect way to judge whether one area had an edge over the other. In later years, that system also was used to give the East or West an extra team, if the ratings judged one of them to be that much better.

Lucia realized his team had beaten Michigan in Ann Arbor earlier in the season, and the NCAA had a history of bringing the host regional team home as a lesser seed. If that happened, Michigan would have to win a game to get to the second round's quarterfinals to play a bye team, and Lucia decided it would be best to play Michigan somewhere other than Ann Arbor. Sure enough, Denver won the West 1 seed, got the bye, but had to face the Michigan-St. Cloud winner in the semifinal, while the Gophers, by getting the West 2 seed and the second bye, wound up playing the Michigan State-Colorado College winner.

The CC Tigers were seeded sixth, and had a tall order to face Michigan State—the almost home team—to get to Minnesota. The Tigers were tough, but in the other bracket, Michigan was the No. 4 seed and beat No. 5 St. Cloud State to jump into the quarterfinals—against Denver. So the Pioneers had to face the Wolverines, in Ann Arbor. Denver coach Gwozdecky, right after his team won the WCHA playoff title, scoffed at the difference. "We look forward to the opportunity," Gwozdecky said. "Playing Michigan at Michigan? Believe me, there's no tougher place to play than Xcel Center when you have to play Minnesota."

Michigan beat St. Cloud State 4-2, while Colorado College ambushed Michigan State 2-0 on Jeff Sanger's shutout. "I think we were confident we could beat CC," said Johnny Pohl. "But we didn't know about Michigan State; they had Ryan Miller, and they play that defensive style. And it was the swan song for their coach (Ron Mason). Then CC goes out and beats 'em."

In the Michigan-St. Cloud State game, Michigan was solidly ahead, but St. Cloud came back, got to within one, then the Huskies scored to tie the game. But the goal was disallowed. Video review showed that a St. Cloud player definitely stepped into crease, but as he did, the puck was already visible, having trickled through the goaltender on the opposite side of the crease. The goal would have made it 3-3, but St. Cloud lost, and Michigan advanced.

Gwozdecky may have rethought his comment about it not being a big deal to face Michigan in Ann Arbor, after his Pioneers had their season rudely ended in a 5-3 loss to Michigan, with the capacity Wolverine crowd screaming its lungs out.

Minnesota did better, battling CC to a 1-1 tie after one period, with Alex Kim's opening goal offset by Grant Potulny. Nick Angell scored a huge power-play goal to break the tie at 8:26 of the second period, and Jeff Taffe put the Gophers up 3-1 58 seconds later. Still, it wasn't easy as the plucky Tigers came back for a goal by Peter Sejna later in the middle period. It all came down to

Pohl, who scored an unassisted shorthanded goal at 5:56 of the final period to secure a 4-2 victory.

Minnesota fired 41 shots at Sanger while CC shot 35 times at Adam Hauser, who blanked CC on all six of its power plays.

"We actually played a really good game against CC," said Pohl. "We outshot em, and we were ahead 3-1, then 3-2 going into the third. We got a shortie. I scored it, six minutes in, to put us up 4-2. We really played smart from then on. With 14 minutes to go, they really didn't get many chances, and they actually took a stupid penalty. We played smart and deserved to win.

"We were pretty pumped up. After the game, I think if anything, our goal was to get to the Frozen Four, because we knew if we got there, anything could happen."

The victory over CC also was the 14th time that the Gophers had won after yielding the first goal.

Jordan Leopold kept a Michigan attacker from threatening to give Adam Hauser time to cover a rebound in the NCAA semifinals.

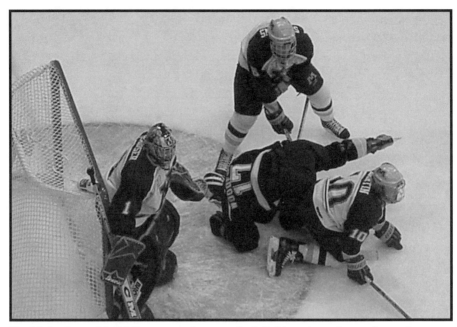

Paul Martin and Judd Stevens took care of a Michigan intruder to the goalmouth, allowing Adam Hauser to maintain his concentration.

Gophers Matt DeMarchi (19), goalie Adam Hauser, Jeff Taffe (27) and Dan Welch (23) reacted after Maine's Robert Liscak had banked in a bad-angle goal for a 3-2 lead with only 4:33 left in the third period.

Chapter 24

At home in St. Paul

IT HAD BEEN A LONG HAUL, but the Gophers were finally making the crosstown trek to the Xcel Energy Center in Saint Paul for the NCAA Frozen Four. There was an interesting side to the usual electrified air surrounding a long-awaited trip to such a tournament, however. These Gophers seemed to be level-headed, not hyper, not even nervous. It was as if they were thrilled to get there—which had been their objective all season, some said—but they also knew there was more to the weekend than just getting there.

"We had a long break," said Johnny Pohl. "We played the NCAA regional quarterfinals on a Saturday, then had 11 days off until the semifinals on Thursday. After the regional, we had two days off, then practiced the next two days, took a day off, practiced for two, took a day off...."

While the Gophers have the luxury of the huge, wide Olympic-sized ice surface at Mariucci Arena—200 feet long and 100 feet wide—the pros play on the standard North American 200 x 85 ice surface. Being 15 feet narrower doesn't seem like such a problem, but it changes the way a player's instincts work. On the bigger ice, a winger breaking wide can keep going, much wider, and turn the corner on a slower defenseman. Meanwhile, a defenseman must be quick and agile to defend against such a winger, while on the narrower ice surface the defenseman can retreat a bit more casually, knowing the winger has to come to him sooner rather than later.

"We practiced at Augsburg to get used to the smaller sheet," said Pohl. "We had good practices. We stayed focused. Nobody was screwing off too much. We had some fun, but we stayed focused. Every once in a while, coach would bring in a letter. He read one that somebody from the 1979 team had sent him. We had the right mindset going in. It was our tournament, our time, and we could beat anybody. We also knew that anybody could beat us."

Coach Don Lucia said he didn't keep the messages, although he appreciated them and he did read them to the players, for whatever effect they might have. The telegram Pohl referred to was from Don Micheletti, who played on the 1979 championship team, the last previous Gopher title team. And it tells a lot about the youthfulness of the Gophers that they listened to his message, but they were too young to have ever heard of Don Micheletti.

"I read a few telegrams, but I didn't keep them," said Lucia, scoffing at the possible historical significance they might hold. "Donny Micheletti sent a really nice one, about how tough it will be. He said whoever we play will be tough, so we've got to be tougher; they'll be fast, so we'll have to be faster; they'll play hard, so we've got to play harder. And that if we've got to be the biggest badasses ever to win, then that's what we've got to be."

Grant Potulny, the only non-Minnesotan who was very much a Minnesotan by that point in the season, said several other important bits of inspiration came from Bob Motzko, the first-year assistant coach. "Motzko brought a lot of energy," said Potulny. "He sat us down one time in February, and told us about how he had been up north somewhere and had a couple beers with a guy from the '79 team, and he went like this...."

With that, Potulny thrust his fist out, about eye-high.

"...With his fist like this, you couldn't miss seeing his NCAA championship ring," Potulny explained. "Then he said to Motzko, 'In 10 years, when you can hold that ring out, it doesn't matter who scored the winning goal.' "

Again, the youthfulness showed. The player in question was Pat Phippen, and he didn't play on the 1979 team, but he did play on both the 1974 and 1976 championship Gopher teams. The great connection with Potulny, who would go on to score the game-winner in overtime in the championship game for the Gophers, is that Phippen scored the clinching goal in the 4-2 championship game triumph over Michigan Tech in 1974, also scored the game-winning goal in the 6-3 victory in the 1976 final.

The lingering impact, almost three decades later, impressed Motzko.

"That was a big part of it all," said Motzko. "I was at a golf thing up at Gull Lake with Pat Phippen, and a group of hockey guys, and I didn't know some of them all that well. I had just been hired, about two weeks earlier. I got introduced to Phip, and he put his fist in my face—with the ring facing me. We talked for about four hours after that. He's a passionate person. It didn't surprise me to find out he was captain of the 1976 team. Part of all this is how it affects guys like that. Those guys wear their rings today, with great pride. You carry that with you all your life.

"That stuck in my mind, all summer, and all through the season," Motzko added. "Finally, I asked if I could talk to the team. I told them I could see this team could be great. They didn't know it, though. I told them that a team is lucky if they get one crack at the championship, and this is your crack."

A senior gets his chance

Both the length of time since the last previous Minnesota NCAA hockey title and the youth of the 2001-02 team's seniors span a large gap in time, which has repeatedly been pointed out. When that last title was won, in 1979, Herb Brooks was coaching; the tournament was played in the old Detroit Olympia and Joe Louis Arena wasn't even built yet; Neal Broten was a freshman; and current Gopher seniors like Nick Angell hadn't been born.

The field was set, with Minnesota taking on Michigan, and Maine playing New Hampshire—the team that had risen to No. 1 in the nation when the top four WCHA teams beat each other up in the stretch drive.

"It's hard to believe, but we're in the Final Four, and I'm so excited I can't wait to get there," said Angell, slipping when he used "Final Four" instead of the politically correct "Frozen Four."

"We're not trying to look at it as us winning the national championship, though," Angell added. "We're looking at it from the standpoint of us playing Michigan. If we win that, then we'll look at the final game."

To recap, it used to be commonplace for Minnesota to be among the final foursome. The Gophers broke through as runner-up in 1971, then gained that elite group 10 times from 1974-89. After winning NCAA titles in 1974, 1976 and 1979, the Gophers were runners-up in 1971, 1975 and 1981. They added final four appearances in 1983 followed by a string of four straight years, in 1986, '87, '88 and '89. They made it again in 1994 and '95, running up their account to 18 trips in 24 years.

But since then, nothing. Angell, who was born seven months after the Gophers won in 1979, only knows that in his years, the Gophers never got close.

"Last year we made our first NCAA regional appearance in my four years," said Angell.

Angell won't disagree that it has been a rocky road to get to this point. The seniors were freshmen when the once-elite Gophers came apart with their second straight sub-.500 season. The next year, after Don Lucia replaced Doug Woog as coach, they dropped from fifth to sixth at 13-13-2 in the WCHA. Even last season, when the Gophers rose to 18-8-2 in the league and made the NCAA regional, it was only for one game.

As a senior, Angell wound up playing solidly throughout, and got a chance to skate on the second power-play unit, through the playoffs.

"I've had kind of an interesting career," said Angell. "Looking back at it, when I was at East, I always scored a lot of points. When I came to Minnesota, my role changed. I became a defensive player because there were other defensemen who got the offensive roles. But I played in 154 games. That's a lot, and I'm proud of it.

"The toughest part was that every year, they wanted the program to improve, so they recruited for guys to make the team, instead of working their way in. So I had to work hard, including every summer, just to make sure I still had a spot to play. I felt that pressure, but I think it actually made me better, the same way as it made everybody better."

Angell stressed that the cohesiveness of the players, from seniors to freshmen, has added a whole new dimension.

"I play with Keith Ballard, and some of the stuff he can do, I think, 'Wow!' And he's only a freshman," Angell said. "He's got so many abilities, it's a nice deal for me to get to work with him. When you look back at our freshman year, about the only contact we had with the seniors was to get our heads shaved."

After UMD upset the Gophers, Angell got a chance to play on the power play the next weekend, against North Dakota. Late in a scoreless game, Angell rifled a slapshot to score the first goal in a 2-1 Minnesota victory. That was it. He stayed on the power play and suddenly his place in the Gopher lineup was solidified. In fact, he was being counted on.

"From top to bottom, with guys like Johnny Pohl, Leopold and Jeff Taffe, I think we've got a great chance in the tournament," Angell said, just before the Frozen Four. "I'm biased, but I think Jordan Leopold should win the Hobey Baker Award. It's been tough some of the time over four years, but I think it's all worked out to be the best, the way everything has come together."

All six seniors shared Angell's sentiments. Pohl assessed the weekend. "It's a no-lose situation, really, just getting there," he said. "Some people probably thought we'd get there, but I don't think anyone was banking on us getting there, all year. Especially the way we played the second half."

Chapter 25

Hauser tames the Wolverines

It was late in the second period of the NCAA Frozen Four semifinals, and University of Minnesota goaltender Adam Hauser faced an easy Michigan shot, which he casually steered away. However, it went right to Jed Ortmeyer, another Michigan attacker, who fired a shot for the open right side of the net. Hauser, diving across the crease, gloved the shot like a shortstop taking away a line-drive single up the middle.

Hauser remembered that save after the game, and it was something like "pre-payback" that he robbed Ortmeyer, who later would score with a bank shot off Hauser with 1:34 remaining. That goal caused the record throng of mostly Gopher fans among the 19,234 at the Xcel Energy Center to hold their collective breath until the Gophers, who had been leading 3-0, could finish off a suddenly-tense 3-2 victory. The victory put Minnesota (31-8-4) into the NCAA championship game against Maine two days later.

"I remember that save," said Hauser. "I was kind of bummed, because I had left a bad rebound on my part. I got across, and was fortunate enough to get that one with my glove. It was just one of those things, because you don't always get those.

"In fact," Hauser added with a chuckle, "for three years I *didn't* get those."

For three rocky seasons, while the once-elite Gophers fluttered between middle of the pack and respectability, Hauser was accused of being the weak link, of providing goaltending that was inadequate for a team that wanted to be a contender. But everything snapped into focus for Hauser and for the Gophers. Just like that key save in the second period, or maybe *because* of that save, the Gophers moved to a position one game away from a shot at their first national championship in 23 years. If they win it, Adam Hauser will be a primary reason.

Asked after the game to list the key factors in the outcome against Michigan, Gopher coach Don Lucia said: "No. 1, Adam Hauser was outstanding tonight. It makes such a difference to be able to play with the lead, and we tried to delay that first Michigan goal for as long as possible."

The crowd of 19,234 broke the Xcel Energy Center record for a college game in Minnesota, and for the arena, and for any hockey game ever held in Minnesota. The record of 19,227 had only lasted about six hours, having been established during the 7-2 Maine victory over New Hampshire in the Thursday afternoon semifinal, which put Maine into the NCAA final from the other bracket.

Hauser and Michigan goaltender Josh Blackburn were tested often, throughout their game, and both made numerous spectacular saves. Through two periods and 13:55 of the third, Hauser was flawless, which gave the Gophers the chance to build a 3-0 lead.

The only goal of the first period was an example. The Gophers attack was stopped, and when a Wolverine defenseman went to clear the puck from behind the net, the puck hit Jeff Taffe in the back of the leg, out in the slot. The carom went right back toward the net, and Grant Potulny swept it in at the crease with 4:20 elapsed.

That got the crowd into the game, and it never really got out of it, offering strong support. The Gophers killed a penalty early in the second period, then got a power play when Michigan was called for too many men on the ice at 3:55. On the power play, John Pohl fed Jordan Leopold, who fired from center-point, and Potulny deftly tipped the puck past Blackburn at 4:33 for a 2-0 lead. The only guy on the Minnesota roster who wasn't from Minnesota had the only two goals in the game.

Hauser came up with one of his two biggest saves shortly after that, when the Wolverines top gunner, Mike Cammalleri, stole the puck and had a clean breakaway. Sailing in off the left boards at full speed, Cammalleri shot low, but Hauser stayed with him and made the save. With Hauser in command, the 2-0 lead looked substantial enough when the third period started, and after just 1:40, it became 3-0 on an all-Hastings play. Dan Welch flipped a pass to spring Taffe on a breakaway, and the lanky junior raced in on Blackburn to score his 34th goal of the season and make it 3-0.

It was some sort of justice for Taffe, who had two or three point-blank chances turned away by Blackburn, and another one that went off the right pipe in the second period.

The Wolverines didn't get to the Frozen Four by being meek or shrinking from a little adversity, however, and they broke Hauser's shutout bid with 6:05 remaining when J.J. Swistak carried up the left side, 1-on-2, while killing a penalty. With a burst of speed, Swistak got by the defense, turned the corner, and veered to the goal-mouth, where he jammed his shot under Hauser.

"The trouble with a 3-0 lead," said Hauser, "is that if they get one, then they just need one more, and they can pull the goalie and tie it. As it was, they pulled the goalie and got it to 3-2."

Sure enough, with 1:34 remaining and Blackburn gone for a sixth attacker, Ortmeyer recovered the puck deep on the left side. He whirled around and flung a pass toward the general area of the crease, and the puck glanced in off Hauser's leg-pad to make it 3-2.

It was a shocker, and it provided a chilling reminder of Hauser's reputation—of making all the tough saves but letting some leaky ones get by. But could it be happening now, in the tight focus of the NCAA tournament? The remaining 1:34 seemed like forever.

"What did I think when it was 3-2?" said Hauser, repeating the question. "I was wishing there were only about five seconds left on the clock. As the game went on, we could tell Michigan would keep pressing. I didn't think we were playing our best hockey right then, and we had to keep making plays, chipping the puck past them."

So they did, and Hauser held firm.

"We played OK," said Pohl, looking back at that NCAA semifinal a month later. "We capitalized. We scored a power-play goal. They made a really bad turnover that we scored on. Jeff got a breakaway and buried it. So it was 3-0 with seven minutes to go. Then they got a shortie on us that they never should have gotten. I don't know how it happened. Adam made one unbelievable save, but that one got in. Then they threw one in from the corner with a minute and a half to go. Everybody thought, 'Oh my god, I can't believe this is happening.' It was a lucky bounce, but I'm sure a lot of people thought, 'Here we go!'

"But once they got the goalie pulled, nothing much happened. And we were on to the championship game."

Nearly 20,000 hearts skipped a beat with 1:34 remaining in the NCAA semifinal game when Michigan scored a wide-angle goal to cut Minnesota's lead to 3-2. Goalie Adam Hauser came back to hold the lead and send the Gophers to the title game

Chapter 26

All-Minnesota, but one

It didn't seem like a big deal, and it wasn't, to many observers. The University of Minnesota hockey team had a player who was not a native of the state of Minnesota, for the first time since Steve MacSwain and John Blue wore the Big M back from 1984-87. The player was Grant Potulny, who was from just across the Red River, in Grand Forks, N.D., so he wasn't far from being a Minnesotan.

The suspicion at the time Potulny was recruited was that he was a token recruit by new coach Don Lucia, to test the waters, and preparatory to him recruiting players from wherever he might find them. Sure enough, right after the Gophers won the NCAA title in 2002, Lucia brought in Thomas Vanek, from Austria, and defenseman Pete Kennedy from Nova Scotia.

It wasn't like Potulny was some sort of ogre. In fact, he fit in well and proved to be a pivotal part of the Gopher championship picture. He was quick to point out that he had been forewarned about potential pressure that might come his way because he wasn't a Minnesotan. It didn't happen, of course. He was accepted by his teammates because of his great work ethic, ability, and personality. And he was accepted by the fans because he was productive and helped win.

"I had been warned about the 'All-Minnesota' team thing," said Potulny. "Steve Johnson, my coach in junior, talked about it with me, and he said 'If you do go there, it will be an issue that you can't get around. There will be a lot of media questions, and are you going to be OK with it?' So I was definitely aware of it. It was sort of a big deal before we started playing, but then we started playing well and people only wanted to talk about the games."

Potulny discussed the all-Minnesota circumstances a few weeks after the tournament was over, and I told him had I still been at the *Minneapolis Star Tribune*, I probably would have been the only member of the media who might have criticized seeing the end of the all-Minnesota concept. Because I was one of the few who had watched it spring to life in the first place.

Most media people saw nothing special about the Gophers being all-Minnesota. Some clamored to end it, buying into the idea that the only reason Minnesota hadn't won any NCAA titles since 1979 was that Minnesota kids no longer could do the job against teams recruited from all over. Others saw it as arrogant, thinking that there was something snooty about these all-Minnesota players thinking they could take on the world. Some of the harshest critics actually suggested that it would be fantastic if Minnesota high school basketball got good enough so that the Gopher basketball team could be made up entirely of Minnesotans—yet they couldn't see any positives for the Gophers to maintain the same thing in hockey.

What I described to Potulny was that because he was from Grand Forks, could he imagine how neat it would be if there were so many players in North Dakota of sufficient skill that the University of North Dakota could be comprised, totally, of North Dakotans? Or, similarly, that Nebraska's football team could be all from Nebraska? The idea is not just to have all-homestaters, but to be good enough to challenge for the national championship with all homestate players.

Potulny understood exactly. The concept was not "anti" anybody, but simply pro-Minnesotan. And it had worked to establish what became known as "*Gopherhockey*" for John Mariucci, Glen Sonmor, and later, especially Herb Brooks.

When Minnesota went to Duluth to face UMD late in the season, I had written a column on the subject. Here is the jist of it:

All-Minnesota Gophers

My first acquaintance with Gopher hockey was back when I was a student, first at UMD, and later at the University of Minnesota. My earliest recollection was how they dressed in all maroon and wore helmets that looked like they had been made from salvaged ham cans. But they skated like crazy, and could always be counted on to over-achieve for coach John Mariucci.

When I transferred to Minnesota to study journalism, I also covered the Gopher hockey team for the Minnesota Daily, the school paper. I went downstairs, into the bowels of the old Williams Arena, where I found Mariucci. It was an intimidating moment, because Mariucci was one of the most rugged characters ever to play in the National Hockey League, and an imposing figure wherever he stood. I approached him apprehensively—and was immediately disarmed from any concerns. John Mariucci was so happy to have any reporter care about hockey, even a student, that he welcomed me with open arms.

Later I went back home to Duluth to start my sports-writing career at the *Duluth News-Tribune*, where I covered everything but focused mainly on high school and college hockey.

It's fun to recall those formative years of the modern (late-1960s) era of college hockey, especially when the Gophers came to Duluth to face UMD at the DECC. I'll never forget when UMD first went to Division I, then moved into the WCHA, then moved into a plush new home, called the Duluth Arena. The Bulldogs' first WCHA game in the new building was against the Gophers. In the game, a pint-sized UMD phenom named Keith (Huffer) Christiansen led the Gophers on a merry chase throughout that game. Invariably, almost like the Pied Piper, he'd lead them away from the net, off toward the corner, then he'd pass to the goal-mouth for a goal. UMD won that game 8-1, and Huffer had six assists—a record that still stands.

It wasn't long after that when Mariucci's regime came to an end, and everybody who ever watched a hockey game in the state was sad. But ol' John landed on his feet, after a fashion, and got a job with the North Stars. I always loved John Mariucci from that first confrontation in the bowels of Williams Arena, and I treasure the fact that I got to know Maroosh well in those later North Stars days, after I went from the *Duluth News-Tribune* to the *Minneapolis Tribune* in the fall of 1967, the year when the North Stars started.

Going back, Maroosh had a dream about Gopher hockey.

The plan was that the University of Minnesota would attempt to block the torrent of 20-year-old hockey imports who were being brought in as freshmen after failing to be drafted and signed by the National Hockey League. These were predominately Canadian junior players from the Tier I or Major Junior leagues in Quebec, Ontario and in Western Canada, because the United States junior programs were insignificant at the time. Mariucci also wanted the Gophers to use Minnesota kids—nurturing and growing these players from obscurity to potential glory, just by providing them with an outlet to play.

In Mariucci's day, it might have been impossible to fill a whole team with just Minnesota kids, so Mariucci did the next best thing. He got the best ones, such as Johnny Mayasich, Dick Dougherty, Jack McCartan and the Meredith brothers, and he filled in with some key imports from Canada, such as Murray Williamson, or Lou Nanne. "I always like to get one Canadian," Mariucci would say, smiling that smile of his that could light up an entire arena, "just to show I don't discriminate."

It became legend that Mariucci refused to play Denver, because Murray Armstrong had armed the Pioneers with all those aging Canadian junior studs. But Mariucci confided to me one day that it never was his idea to boycott Denver, but athletic director Marsh Ryman's order. Mariucci was staunchly against bringing in 21-year-old freshmen, rather than 18- or 19-year-olds, and while he also may have opposed the concept of importing all the players, he never—ever—would have passed up the opportunity to take 'em on, and try to beat them.

When Wisconsin went big-time in hockey, Mariucci tried to get Bob Johnson to do the same thing in Wisconsin, to nurture Wisconsin's high school system as development ground. But Badger Bob was too impatient, too eager to get to the glory years, so he went deeply into Canada for the vast majority of his talent. The Badgers won, for sure, and nobody would criticize Badger Bob for how quickly he built an elite program there, but high school hockey in Wisconsin still languishes, in quality and quantity, compared to Minnesota, which still ranks at the top among hockey-producing states, because of the fantastic and competitive high school programs.

It's a difference in scope. A difference in ideals. A difference in dreams.

Mariucci's dream was a dream that Sonmor, a Canadian, believed in reverently. So did Herb Brooks. Brad Buetow followed and didn't adhere to the dream quite as totally, but Doug Woog—who played for Mariucci—came in and strengthened Mariucci's fondest wishes.

A whole lot of very good athletes have played hockey somewhere in Minnesota, and especially in Northern Minnesota, and a primary reason might have been that colleges, and pro teams, came here looking for standouts once they finally realized that Minnesotans could play the game. Under Sonmor, Brooks, Buetow and Woog, the Gophers became a stronghold of home-state talent. As Mariucci would say, proudly, "I'm not anti-Canadian, just pro-Minnesotan." When Brooks won his NCAA championships, every player on the team was from Minnesota.

Woog's teams were the same, although they never won a title. But they challenged, annually. Meanwhile, there were enough great players to go elsewhere, to help North Dakota, Wisconsin, Colorado College and UMD rise to the top. Don Lucia starred at Grand Rapids, then at Notre Dame, while assistant Mike Guentzel was a top defenseman at Greenway of Coleraine, then at

Minnesota. Assistant Bob Motzko came out of Austin, Minn., by way of St. Cloud State. UMD head coach Scott Sandelin played at Hibbing, then went to North Dakota. His first assistants were Steve Rohlik and Mark Strobel, both of whom were stars at Hill-Murray and wound up as captains of different teams at Wisconsin.

Wherever they went, they could find a place to play. All the rest of the college hockey programs in the country were made up from players assembled from wherever the coaches could find prospects, but the Gophers were all-Minnesota. The University of Minnesota program remained the exclusive territory for Minnesota prospects to realize the dream they had been dreaming since they first strapped on skates as kids. It was John Mariucci's dream, and it lived on, even after John died.

Others resented it. Cynics said the Gophers didn't recruit, they selected, because there were so many outstanding Minnesota players and they all wanted mostly to go play for Minnesota. The Gophers never really flaunted it, but there was an undercurrent of extra determination to live up to a higher standard because you were playing with the guys you grew up playing against. To get a chance to play in the Gopher lineup was to be one of the few players who were asked to play on this impromptu homestate select team.

When Don Lucia was coaching in his final season at Colorado College, and the Minnesota program seemed to be coming apart, he asked me if I thought a "non-M-Man" could be accepted as a Gopher coach. I told him he—Lucia—could, because he was from Minnesota, he understood the traditions, and once there, he would find out how special it was to be…well, special. And, I added, I was certain he would adopt the principles and standards that upheld John Mariucci's dream.

Donny got the job, and he will be successful. He may even win NCAA championships with the Gophers, something nobody other than Brooks has achieved. But things have changed. In the Gopher yearbook, Lucia is quoted as explaining that he is asked about his recruiting policy more than anything else. He acknowledges his answer won't make everybody happy. "We are looking at kids from throughout the world," Lucia says. "…Eventually there will be quite a few recruits from outside the state, and possibly outside the country as well."

There's a player here, and a recruit or two there, who have been brought in purposely from outside the state of Minnesota. OK. The players being brought in are exceptional, I'm sure. Maybe even better than the player, or players, from Minnesota who grew up dreaming of being a Gopher. But maybe not, too. With a total of 18 scholarships available, every kid from outside the state who becomes a Gopher hockey player means one less homestate player who will get a chance to fulfill a dream that he shared, spanning across generations, with John Mariucci.

What the new coaching staff, and administration, doesn't seem to realize is that the Gopher hockey program used to be so special that there were two distinctly different types of college hockey programs: One was "*Gopherhockey*," and the other was "Everybody Else."

The Gopher hockey program now is very good again, but the choice has been made. It has become less like the "*Gopherhockey*" of Maroosh's dream, and it has become more like "Everybody Else."

Matt Koalska, left, and Grant Potulny—roommates, coconspirators and scorers of the two biggest goals of Minnesota's season—relaxed on the steps of their apartment while reflecting on the championship season. Koalska tied the Maine game in the final minute, and Potulny scored the overtime game-winner.

Chapter 27

Getting ready
(Hobey Friday)

After the Thursday semifinal victory over Michigan, the Gophers had one full day to wait before the Saturday final. NCAA tournament procedure has evolved to the point that Friday has become the day the Hobey Baker Memorial Award is presented. When the Decathlon Club in Bloomington first came up with the idea for the Hobey Baker Award, I was honored to be a part of the original panel of voters. I had suggested to their board members that to establish it, the award should be voted on and then presented at the NCAA tournament in order to command maximum exposure, and that was put into place.

After several years, when the award was well-established, I then urged the Decathlon Club organizers to switch it to the weekend after the NCAA tournament, where it could well stand on its own. My reasoning was that often the award goes to a player who is going to play in the national championship game the next day, and the award adds a measure of undue pressure that is unfair to the player, and could lead to criticism for the selection if the player happens to have less than his best game in the final because of the extra pressure.

For historical perspective, Mike Motteau of Boston College won it in 2000, and BC lost to North Dakota in the final; Jason Krog of New Hampshire won in 1999, and UNH lost to Maine the next day in the final.

But in 2002, the Hobey became the perfect way for the Minnesota hockey players to spend Friday afternoon, on NCAA final eve. Jordan Leopold won the award, and the Gophers were able to use it as a positive distraction.

Leopold was properly honored, and personally thrilled, but he remained humble. And the award as the top player in college hockey was always kept in perspective.

"I've gotten a lot of individual awards, going back to since I was a little kid," said Leopold. "But I never won a big championship with a team."

Leopold and Pohl remained in tight duo of mutual admiration. Proud as he was to win the Hobey, Leopold couldn't understand how Pohl could not be at least a finalist. And Pohl simply said there was no way he could win the award because Leopold was the best.

"Everyone on our team thought Jordan should win it, that he was the best player," said Pohl. "But there was a little doubt, so when he won, everybody on our team was so happy—so genuinely happy—for him. I think that's a testament to how great of a guy, how great a leader and what kind of teammate Jordan is."

As for the potential distraction, Pohl scoffed.

"Go back to the Denver game at the Final Five," he said. "Losing to Denver focused us a lot more. I think it focused our guys more than we realized, that it wasn't going to be a walk in the park, that we have to be ready. We stayed focused the rest of the way, even on that Friday, with the Hobey Baker thing. We had practice; had a good time at the Hobey, but everybody stayed focused. We went out to eat as a team, came back and had a little meeting. We just kind of talked. We had everything worked out."

Hauser faces final test

So it has come down to this for Adam Hauser. It will take a great performance in the final game of his four-year collegiate hockey career to validate Hauser as a worthy goaltender.

Ridiculous though it may be, Hauser has heard continued criticism, bordering on abuse, for more than three seasons about how he had let down the Gophers with erratic play and the tendency to allow a shaky goal or two. The criticism has been so steady that even now, as a senior, cynics are waiting for Hauser to collapse and take the Gophers down with him.

But at 6 p.m. today in the Xcel Energy Center in Saint Paul, the Gophers (31-8-4) will try to win their first NCAA hockey championship in 23 years, and if they beat Maine (26-10-7) to accomplish that feat, Adam Hauser will have to play a primary role. And if he does, he will set a record for WCHA goaltending victories. Does that sound like someone who should still have to prove himself?

Hauser's flawless goaltending allowed Minnesota to stake out a 3-0 lead in Thursday's 3-2 semifinal victory over Michigan. That turned out to be Hauser's 82nd victory over four seasons—tying him with Ron Grahame, the Denver star of the 1960s, for the most career victories in the WCHA. After finishing his college career on a 12-1 roll since February 1, the critics might still be out there, but they no longer seem to bother Hauser.

"I don't know what anybody else is thinking, but I can't stop what they're thinking," said Hauser. "Finally, I've learned that it doesn't matter what other people are thinking. I pretty much stopped reading the papers. But definitely, I couldn't deal with it very well in my first three years."

An examination of the record book indicates that much of the criticism from those first three years might have been invalid. True, there were breakdowns, but the Gophers themselves were coming unglued in the last year of Doug Woog's coaching regime—Hauser's first year. He was thrust into the nets full-time, as an 18-year-old.

Hauser, from Bovey, had played at Greenway of Coleraine High School, but left to go to the USA Hockey development camp at Ann Arbor, where high-school age players play the equivalent of a junior hockey schedule. So with that as accelerated development, it seemed that the jump to the WCHA might not be so bad, but the team struggled, and Hauser struggled with the pressure. Hauser was 14-18-8 for that freshman season, with a 3.47 goals-against average and an .876 save percentage. Not good.

As a sophomore, he was 20-14-2, with a 2.95 goals-against and a .909 save percentage. Last season, Hauser was 26-12-2 with a 2.56 goals-against and a .902 save percentage. Those marks are very good, but the haunting problem was that the Gophers continued to allow surprisingly easy goals—the kind critics call "bad goals"—at inopportune times.

Through it all, he kept working to improve. And if he had experienced an emotional rollercoaster, he also acquired a new goalie coach in Robb Stauber. The former Duluth Denfeld goaltender who went on to win the Hobey Baker award in 1998, and led the Gophers to the NCAA final at the St. Paul Civic Center, where they lost a brilliantly played 4-3 overtime game to Harvard in the 1989 title game. Stauber also is one of the most stable goaltenders ever to pull on a mask, and it would appear that stability has rubbed off on Hauser over the past two years.

Hauser enters the NCAA championship game with these stats: 22-6-4, goals-against average of 2.40, with a stunning .920 save percentage. Hauser had stifled Colorado College in the NCAA regional, to send the Gophers to Xcel Center where he beat Michigan in the semifinals.

"He was great last week, and he was great again tonight," said Stauber after Hauser beat Michigan. "He's playing so consistently that I haven't said a word of instruction to him in three weeks.

"He was sharp—but calm. I told him to think of some of your best games, where you were calm, and duplicate that feeling."

Being calm is important to Stauber, who always seemed calm, and it is something that is new and different for Hauser. He remained calm against Michigan, even when Wolverine Eric Nystrom took a serious run at him and blatantly bodychecked him into the goal during the third period of the semifinal. There was no penalty on the play, but Hauser remained unruffled.

"Yeah, it was pretty blatant," said Hauser. "But it wasn't totally unjustified. I had caught him a little off-guard when he came by the net a little while before that. So he was probably a little upset."

Coach Don Lucia credited Hauser with giving the Gophers a chance to take charge against Michigan. Asked about the difference between the Hauser of the last three seasons and the Hauser who had gone 12-1 since February, Lucia said: "Adam has been very good when he's had to be, and he's been that way the whole second half of the season. I think the big thing about Adam is that he's been able to mature, and he's been better every year.

"I think he's also been able to keep the big picture. He's fresh, excited, and happy. When he's on top of his game, he's aggressive, and he looks big in the net. On top of everything else, he's a great kid—there's not a finer young man. I'm really happy for him."

Maine, of course, presents some tough challenges. The Black Bears are riding a crest of emotion to win the title for Shawn Walsh, the coach who recruited them all, put them all together, kept coaching them through last season while undergoing therapy for cancer, and died from the disease on the day before practice started. Under coach Tim Whitehead and assistant Grant Standbrook, the Black Bears battled to stay in contention in Hockey East, battling Boston University in a race for second behind New Hampshire.

The Bears were seeded third in the East behind New Hampshire and Boston University, and after beating Harvard 4-3 in overtime to open the East Regional, Maine beat Boston University 4-3 to get to the Frozen Four, where they embarrassed top-ranked New Hampshire 7-2 Thursday. Having eliminated the two Hockey East teams seeded ahead of them, the Black Bears now are after bigger game.

Minnesota has some of the best individually skilled players in the country, including centers Johnny Pohl, who has 26 goals and Jeff Taffe, who has 34, and defenseman Jordan Leopold, who has 20 goals and was just named winner of the Hobey Baker Award. The Black Bears, however, were tenacious throughout Thursday's 7-2 blitzing of New Hampshire. They are led by Colin Shields, who has 29 goals, Niko Dimitrakos, who has 20, and defenseman

Peter Metcalf, who has 9 goals and provides added emotional support by carrying out the Shawn Walsh jersey to the Maine bench every game. The Black Bears also have Matt Yeats in goal, backed up by Mike Morrison—both seniors.

"Maine has a great team," said Lucia. "Both teams are kind of in the same boat. Both finished third in their league, both lost in their league playoff final, and both have senior goaltenders. It's a great match-up. It might be an advantage to Maine that this will be the third Frozen Four for some of them."

For the Gophers—every one of them—it's the first Frozen Four. And with Adam Hauser on top of his game, it's the only one they care about.

If goalie Adam Hauser and Gopher defensemen Keith Ballard (13) and Nick Angell were surprised by a Black Bear prowling in Minnesota's crease in the NCAA final, it was only temporary—and Hauser found ways to get even.

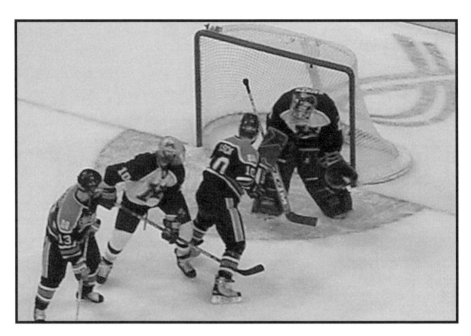

Goalie Adam Hauser had different levels of protection against Maine, finding only Paul Martin trying to engage two Maine attackers while he kept a Maine shot smothered without allowing a rebound (above) one time; and finding all five teammates helping out to keep the Black Bears from threatening (below) on another occasion.

Chapter 28

Sudden end to classic final

MAYBE COACH DON LUCIA WAS RIGHT. Lucia determined that the University of Minnesota hockey team couldn't win a national championship with just Minnesota players, so he recruited the first of what will be more out-of-staters by bringing in Grant Potulny, from Grand Forks, N.D. For two years, Potulny proved his worthiness, but never any more than he did on a Saturday night at the Xcel Energy Center in Saint Paul. Potulny paid dividends beyond Lucia's most optimistic dreams, as the hard-nosed sophomore winger knocked in a rebound at 16:58 of sudden-death overtime to give the Gophers a 4-3 victory over Maine in the NCAA championship game.

The victory brought Minnesota its first NCAA title since 1979, and it came before 19,324 fans at Xcel Energy Center—the largest crowd ever to watch a hockey game in the state—and it gave the Gophers a 32-8-4 final record to Maine's 26-11-7. The chance for victory had to be gained in the final minute of regulation, when Matt Koalska intercepted a clearing attempt and fired a screened 35-footer that glanced in off goaltender Matt Yeats's stick with 53 seconds remaining.

"I scored a whopping 10 goals this year," said Koalska. "I scored big goals with the Vulcans, but that doesn't compare. This time I got a chance to score and put us in overtime, to give us a chance to win it."

The winning goal became controversial because referee Steve Pietrowski appeared to put his whistle away while several obvious infractions occurred, as is traditional in overtime games. Then he called Maine's Michael Schutte for tripping after an attempted bodycheck on, of all people, Koalska at center ice, 15:58 into the overtime.

"It was a pretty big call," said Koalska. "We were playing at home, and things kind of went our way. But the guy tripped me. He stepped up, I looked up because a bunch of guys on the bench yelled, 'Heads up!' I tried to dipsy-do around him, but we hit knee-to-knee. I think if I'd gotten around him, it would have been a breakaway."

Instead, Koalska went flying, and Pietrowski called tripping. Offered the extra man, the Gophers connected. Jordan Leopold, who was named Hobey Baker Award winner one day earlier, shot from the right point. The puck hit Maine's Francis Nault and landed amid several feet in the scramble at the crease. Johnny Pohl and Nault both swung at it but couldn't connect. Then Potulny gave it a try and put it past Yeats, bringing the big crowd to its feet and sending the Gophers off the bench for a mob scene on the ice.

"I swatted it, and it went between the goalie's legs," said Potulny.

Yeats followed the flight of the puck as it approached. "The defenseman (Leopold) wristed it in diagonally in front of the goal," said Yeats. "It hit our defenseman, and the puck fell and they whacked at it, and it got under me."

Maine coach Tim Whitehead tried to deflect the criticism. "I liked how we played, as the game went on," he said. "They won because they battled back, and our hats are off to them. The crowd was awesome. It was really fun to play in front of a crowd like that."

When pressed, Whitehead said: "I really don't want to make a big deal out of the ref's call. I was a little surprised by the call, because there hadn't been any other calls in the overtime. Had it been in the offensive zone on a clear scoring chance, it would have been a good call. Unfortunately, the game-winning goal came on a power play in overtime. That's frustrating, especially for our players."

The Black Bears were obviously bitter about the penalty, and it was more than just being hard losers. Captain Peter Metcalf said: "I think the guy had it out for us. He's the same guy who threw Coach (Shawn) Walsh out last year, and it was a mistake by the NCAA to put him in this game."

Pietrowski, from the CCHA, ejected Walsh from the 3-1 loss to Boston College at Worcester, Mass., in last spring's East Regional. Maine's players insist that Walsh's ejection came after a comparatively mild protest about a call. In any event, that early departure came in the last game Walsh ever coached. Walsh died of cancer the day before practice began last fall, which elicited a surge of emotional support that became the focal point for the Black Bears all season. A Maine game jersey, with "WALSH" lettered on the back, was carried out to hang above the bench at every Maine game.

However, power play or not, someone still had to put the winning goal into the net, and who better than Potulny, the hard-nosed sophomore who always seems to be in the right place when there's action in front of the net.

In the media interview room after the game, before Potulny could respond to a question about being the only nonMinnesotan on the Gopher roster, he was given an immediate round of applause from Pohl, Leopold and goaltender Adam Hauser, who were also seated at the head table.

Hauser had committed one of those obvious overtime infractions when he swung his goalie stick to trip Maine's Robert Liscak and sent him sprawling into the corner. "It didn't look like there would be a lot of penalties called," said Hauser. "It was his judgment, and you can't argue too much with it, because it won't do you any good. But we put it away at the end."

Hauser made 42 saves as the Black Bears outshot Minnesota 45-35, and he was named all-tournament along with Pohl, Potulny and Maine's Liscak and defensemen Peter Metcalf and Michael Schutte. Potulny, after two goals against Michigan meant he scored three of Minnesota's seven Frozen Four goals, was named tournament most valuable player.

Pietrowski gave the Black Bears the first three penalties in the game, and the Gophers gained a 1-0 lead on the first of those power plays when Keith Ballard worked a give-and-go maneuver with Troy Riddle while moving in from the point to score from the slot at 7:18 of the opening period.

Schutte tied it 1-1 on a Maine power play at 4:47 of the second, after Metcalf faked a shot from left point and instead passed to Schutte, wide open at the right of the net. But just 51 seconds later, Pohl rushed up the left side and snapped a hard wrist shot from the top of the left circle that beat Yeats's glove to the upper right corner to reclaim the lead for Minnesota at 2-1.

Maine, however, came back strong, appearing to take command by outshooting the Gophers 13-8 in the second session, and 16-9 in the third. Still, it wasn't until the third period that the Black Bears could get their second goal past Hauser. Schutte's quick shot from center point caught the right edge of the net at 1:17 for a 2-2 tie. It stayed that way until only 4:33 remained. And, sure enough, the Black Bears stuck a strange goal past Hauser.

With the big crowd sensing overtime, Niko Dimitrakos shot the puck in wide to the left of the net, and Liscak raced in after it, beyond the goal line on the left. He got to it, and abruptly whirled and flung the puck toward the crease. It hit Hauser's pad and glanced in for a 3-2 Maine lead.

One last, cruel, weird goal.... Would that become Adam Hauser's legacy? With the final four minutes ticking away, it certainly seemed like it.

"People say that was another of those easy goals," said Hauser. "I hear that all the time. The thing I had with the goal against Maine, whoever shot the puck, it went wide, and this other guy was screaming in at 30 miles an hour. It was a race, between this guy coming after the puck and for me to get back to the post. I had just gotten done fronting with the save, and I had to turn around and get back to the post. The kid made a fabulous play. Whether he was trying to score or just throwing it on the net, only he will know."

Nonetheless, when the game got down to its final minute, it looked like just one more of those heart-breaking losses for the Gophers to file away.

There was an icing with 58.3 seconds showing, and Lucia summoned Hauser to the bench for a sixth attacker. He sent out Pohl's line, with Koalska as the extra man. Koalska, with so many players jamming the slot for the right-corner faceoff, decided to hang back just a bit. When the puck was dropped, Pohl actually didn't win the faceoff, but the puck hit a couple of skates and wound up squirting to the slot. Tommy Reimann, a Maine junior from Blaine, dived and tried to swat the loose puck out of the zone. But his attempt at game-winning heroics took an unlikely twist when the puck went right at Koalska, who blocked it, stepped in and fired a quick one-timer that somehow found its way through a maze of bodies and through Yeats to tie the game with just under 53 seconds showing.

"There were 52.4 seconds left," said Koalska. "In that situation, you get a chance, and you let it go. You get all kinds of chances during the game, then you get a chance like that, and you let it rip. It went through a skate and stick and headed for the 5-hole, like the puck had eyes or something."

"I didn't see the puck," said Yeats. "It hit my stick and went through my legs."

Pohl said: "Maine really took it to us a lot of the game, and Adam bailed us out. Maine could have won, and maybe deserved to win, but we got what was maybe a lucky bounce on Koalska's goal. When we scored the tying goal, people said they thought the roof was going to blow off."

Hauser, on the bench after being pulled, said: "It's hard to sit there on the bench and watch our six guys try to score. When we scored, I felt great, but I felt the job was not quite done. I had the feeling it would be a long time before the winning goal would be scored."

He was right. Some of the Gophers said they thought they might score again and win it before the final 53 seconds could elapse. With 41 seconds to go, Matt DeMarchi and Lucas Lawson jousted, and were awarded coincidental hitting-after-the-whistle penalties. Regulation ended uneventfully, and then came overtime. With Hauser chopping down a couple of Maine forwards, without being called, everyone assumed there would be no more penalties. Hauser nailed another Maine skater, and several other things that could have passed as infractions also were overlooked.

Hauser stopped a 2-on-1, and Yeats stopped Troy Riddle's backhander. Through 15:58 of sudden-death overtime, those were probably the best chances. At that moment, Koalska broke up ice and looked back for a pass. Michael Schutte stepped up, timing his move for a bodycheck to coincide with the arrival of the puck. Koalska looked up and jumped to the side, but didn't quite miss knee-to-knee contact. Koalska sprawled, Pietrowski blew his whistle, and Schutte went to the penalty box.

Various Gopher players shrugged and accepted the penalty as justified, although Jordan Leopold showed some empathy. "I was kind of hoping we wouldn't get a goal on the power play," said Leopold. "I wanted it to be fair and square."

Exactly one minute later, Pohl won a right-corner faceoff, and Leopold didn't get good wood on his shot.

"It wasn't even on net!" Leopold said. "It certainly wasn't planned. When Pohl got the puck back to me at the point, I'm thinking, 'Don't turn it over.' Because if you turn it over in that situation, you'd never get over it. So I shot, and I remember it was wide of the net and it hit their guy in front of the net."

The puck fluttered wide to the left of the goal and hit a Maine defenseman in the midsection, then fell to the ice, 10 feet out from the goal. Everybody swung at it, but only Potulny connected.

"I was going to front of the net," said Potulny. "Leopold shot, and the puck hit their D. Johnny whiffed on it, and the goalie went down and opened his legs up, because he thought Johnny was going to bring it. I just swung at it, and the puck had eyes."

Leopold, still back at the right point, and greatly relieved he had gotten his shot away and into the thick of traffic at the net, wasn't sure what happened in the chaos in front.

"The puck landed right there, and both Johnny and Grant had a shot at it," said Leopold. "I didn't know what happened, but I saw the red light go on, and we went crazy."

The Gophers swarmed off the bench and piled onto each other in a spontaneous outburst, while the huge crowd stood and cheered for several long minutes after the game had ended, and reality had set in. The Gophers were national champs.

"We found out how hard it is to win this," said Lucia, noting the fragile nature of such games by recalling the last time Minnesota had played Maine, a year earlier, in the NCAA Regional. "Last year, we got the penalty and Maine scored," said Lucia. "This year, they got the penalty and we scored. It was our time. I think we believed it."

The whole country had to believe it.

Four attackers swarmed Maine goalie Matt Yeats as John Pohl (9), Barry Tallackson (27) and Matt Koalska (24) were joined by defenseman Jordan Leopold.

Grant Potulny (18) thrust his stick in the air almost as soon as his shot hit the back of the net to give Minnesota a 4-3 victory over Maine at 16:58 of sudden-death overtime in the NCAA final, as Johnny Pohl (9) and Jeff Taffe (22) reacted.

Chapter 29

Two enormous goals

THE FINAL SEASON FOR SENIORS JOHNNY POHL, Jordan Leopold, Adam Hauser, Nick Angell, Pat O'Leary and Erik Wendell couldn't have been better or more satisfying, and it all makes a great story, the way they came through right to the finish, supplying the fabric of the championship.

But when the 2002 title game story gets told and retold, the focus will remain on two goals by underclassmen that created the startling turnaround—the amazing tying goal by Matt Koalska with 53 seconds remaining in the third period, and the opportunistic winning goal by Grant Potulny after 16:58 of overtime.

Potulny's quick work with the rebound of a Leopold point shot was not the most classic goal ever scored, but it was a thing of beauty to Gopher fans everywhere. It wouldn't have been possible, however, without the last-minute heroics of Koalska at the end of regulation time. Koalska, always effervescent, went back over what he can call "*the* goal."

"We pulled the goalie, and had a 6-on-5 in the last minute," said Koalska. "We took a time out, Motzko and Looch said who should play where. They had it all planned.... You know, you can draw it up, but it never works out that way. Johnny would be taking draw, Riddle would be here, on the half-boards, Leo there, Jeff over there and Paulie out there....

"So we went out there. Johnny took the draw, but he actually didn't really win it. It was pretty much a toss-up. Riddle was over on the half-boards, but there were so many people in front, I thought, 'Maybe I'll stay back, just in case it pops out.' And it popped out, right on my tape. It was quick. Riddle and their guy were fighting for the puck. For me, it was easy. Somehow, they were both going after it, trying to hit the puck. It was one of those goals where you just kind of shoot it.

"You see where you are, where the net is, and let it go. It went through a skate, through a stick, then through the 5-hole. It hit his stick, then went up. I shot it on the ice, for the 5-hole, then it went up in the air, halfway up the net. Must have hit the goalie's stick. I don't know how it went up in the air. Fifty-two-point-four seconds left."

Potulny said it helped to have a miracle working, too. "Assistant Coach Bobby Motzko had said he'd been involved with teams with more talent that didn't win, and way less talent that did win. He thought we had the right mix, the right chemistry," Potulny said. "But when there's 52 seconds left, you need a miracle, pretty much. People can talk all they want about comebacks, and teams that can come back. But when there's 52 seconds left, you need a miracle."

Enter, Koalska.

"As much as Coach Lucia said he didn't think the crowds would be an advantage, I thought it was," said Pohl. "There were 21,000 there, 20,000 for us, and 1,000 for the other team. We were playing, it was the opportunity of a lifetime, and it was *loud!*

"In the last minute of regulation, I was taking the draw," Pohl added. "I actually did win the draw, but as I'm pulling it back, it hits my skate. It sits there for a while, and actually goes toward their net. Not fast at all. One of their guys chops it, but Koalska one-times it. Probably their goalie was screened by everybody."

As for the move to put Koalska, a 9-goal scorer for the season, out there with the goalie pulled, Pohl smiled. "He had to put Koalska out there, he was awesome," said Pohl. "He definitely had played his best game that night. After the puck went to the slot, I was trying to get to the net. I thought, 'Maybe I can get a rebound.' But it went right in. Unbelievable! We hadn't done that in so long. When we got that goal, a lot of our guys thought we could win it in regulation."

If Koalska's tying goal was the result of some sort of karma, it could have come from conversations he had had with Potulny, his roommate. Nobody has scored a higher percentage of big goals than Potulny, and the two had commiserated with each other about what a tough year they both had in scoring. Koalska, who went from Hill-Murray to play for the St. Paul Vulcans, had scored 20-50—70 his senior year in high school, and led the Vulcans with 30-40—70 in 72 games. He scored 10 goals as a freshman at Minnesota, but he only scored 10 goals again as a sophomore. Not that it mattered, as long as he timed No. 10 just right.

Potulny, meanwhile, spent the same two seasons establishing himself as the scorer of big goals, in big games. He scored usually by deft tip-ins or quick reaction to rebounds, and the significance of those goals was far more important than the total might indicate. He scored 22-11—33 as a freshman, with 16 of those 22 goals on power plays, and five of his goals were game-winners. The Gophers, who had a 27-13-2 record for the 2000-01 season, were 17-2-1 in games where Potulny had at least one point. That means they were 10-11-1 when he didn't score. One of the losses the Gophers suffered when he did score was the 4-3 loss to Maine in the NCAA Regional to end the 2000-01 season, and Potulny scored twice in that game.

As a sophomore, Potulny scored 15-19—34, indicating one more point but seven fewer goals than his freshman term. But while his goal total dipped to 15, eight of them on power plays, Potulny scored four goals in the three NCAA tournament games, when he was named all-tournament and most valuable player. Strangely enough, Potulny failed to score a single point in two WCHA Final Five tournaments, and he has no assists in four NCAA tournament games over two seasons. But in those four NCAA games, including the loss to Maine in his freshman year, Potulny has six goals. And while he scored only three game-winners as a sophomore, they included the game-winner in the game that mattered most.

"I scored 15 goals all year, and obviously, that last one was the biggest one," said Potulny. "You know what was nice was that all year the puck hadn't been going in. Individually I didn't have a good year, scoring-wise. But for some reason, everything works out in the end. We talked about that, too, me and the Polack [Koalska]. We said, 'You know, we'll get some at the end when we need 'em.' And we did."

It took the controversial penalty call to set the stage, however, with Maine's Michael Schutte called for tripping at 15:58 of overtime. On the play, Koalska was skating out fast and looking back for an outlet pass when Schutte stepped up. They hit, Schutte's left knee to Koalska's right knee, and Koalska went flying.

That provided the pivotal power play. On the game-winning play, Pohl had pulled the right-corner faceoff back to Leopold, then Pohl broke for the net, as did Potulny.

"At the end of the game, Tom Reimann was on the draw against me," said Pohl. "It was on the same side, the right corner, my side on the draw. Same as on tying goal. I won the draw, and got it back to Jordan, and I thought, 'Oh my god, we might win it on the draw.' Jordan took a shot, but the goalie kicked it to the side. Taffe got it in the corner, did this little Jeff-Taffe-stickhandling move, and threw it out to the point. Jordan shot—a *bad* shot. Their defenseman got hit with it in the stomach. It was a bad shot, but it shows, you throw it at the net, you never know what can happen. The puck dropped right down. I saw it. And I swatted at it, and their D swung at the same time. Our sticks hit, and neither of us got the puck. The puck went right to Grant, and he swatted it in.

"I thought, 'Oh…. My…. God!' I couldn't believe it. I was happy he scored. Glad to see it."

Maine goalie Matt Yeats flinched to make a reactionary save while Grant Potulny – who else? – tried to sneak past the defense.

Matt Koalska never let things like defensemen, goaltenders or the law of gravity prevent him from getting to the net.

Matt DeMarchi (left) fired a shot through the gathering Maine defense as Dan Welch (top) and Jake Fleming (29) looked for a rebound.

The Gophers poured off the bench to celebrate the moment they had worked for all season, moments after Grant Potulny's overtime game-winning goal gave them a 4-3 victory over Maine and their first NCAA national championship in 23 years.

Chapter 30

Golden afterglow

SOME KEY ELEMENTS of the NCAA championship game were easy to overlook in view of the two enormous goals that pulled victory from defeat. Among them were a couple of free-chopping acts by goaltender Adam Hauser in overtime. There were a lot of views, particularly after the later penalty on Maine would contribute to setting up Minnesota's power-play winner.

"In the first period, we took the game over," recalled Koalska. "It's a game of momentum. You know it's going to shift, that we'd both have it for a while. In the second period, they took it over. In the third period, they dominated it right to the end. They were doing it all for Walsh. But when we scored, it seemed like it had to be our game.

"Then we get into overtime, and on the first shift, Hauser chops the guy down. Then Leo goes and gets the puck in our end, and Howie gives another guy a shot at the side of the net."

Leopold laughed about it. "Hauser doesn't worry about other people protecting him, he protects himself," said Leopold. "It's a good thing sometimes.... He got away with two of them. I skated up to him and said, 'Cmon, we're in overtime in the national championship game. Don't make yourself a headline.' "

Hauser knew he was playing the odds. "The Maine guy was coming in pretty fast," he said. "I'm covering, and I didn't chop him *that* hard. It was a very isolated incident, and it has become a big deal because it got caught on video by ESPN. For every time I checked somebody, there were a lot of other things going on, and he didn't call anything. I'm watching our forwards beat the living snot out of their D, to the extent Maine had to hold and hook.

"That's the reason the guy called the penalty in overtime.... It could have been a career-ending knee injury," added Hauser, who was ignited as brightly as all his teammates after the winning goal.

"I've seen it happen before," he said. "Against CC in my sophomore year, we were in the playoffs and we scored and won in overtime. The second game, we beat CC and knocked them out. But those comebacks are far and few between. As for the winning goal, I don't like to watch that closely at the other end, and I wasn't this time. I'm thinking, 'Shoot the puck.' I know there were a zillion guys in front. I hate that."

Pohl shrugged off the irregularity of the questionable penalty calls.

"I think everybody points at the one where Hauser chopped their guy down," said Pohl. "But there was a lot of stuff going on. Had we not scored, it was coming right back on us, he would have called one on us right away. In the first five minutes of overtime, you probably can get away with murder. But after a while, everyone knows you have to call something. Which would you rather have, a penalty, or a guy going in alone on a breakaway?"

Pohl was referring to the Maine penalty, on which, incidentally, the victim was none other than Koalska, helping to set up his roomie's goal.

A month after the championship had been won, Pohl and the other Gophers were still aglow.

"I've only watched it once on videotape," said Pohl. "We smoked em in the first period, but didn't have much to show for it. It was only 1-0, and they were definitely in the game. Then they completely turned it around. Their goals were rewards for outworking us. Eventually, the wall was going to crack. It cracked for us."

But it also was time to reflect on the entire season. After it was over, and all the big plays and the big games had been evaluated, it seems that the majority felt that the WCHA playoff final against Denver was the key game to the entire season for Minnesota. After 32 victories, many of them scintillating, most of the Gophers looked back on the only loss Minnesota suffered in the final 11-1 surge as the key result. The Gophers had won eight straight before that loss, and they won all three NCAA playoff games after the loss.

"The best thing that happened to us was losing to Denver," said Pohl. "Losing that game meant we had to refocus, to rethink where we were at. There comes a point where you have to regroup. We hadn't lost for a while, and we had to come back down, because we had two weeks to get ready for the NCAAs. I hardly ever get overconfident, and even I was overconfident for that game against Denver."

Freshman Keith Ballard, who is from Baudette—pronounced "B'dette," incidentally, and not "BAW-dett"—agreed that the Gophers were on a great roll, but it might have been tough to continue it until the end. "Denver, St. Cloud, and CC...they were all tough, although it's not like they were on a pedestal, in our own minds," said Ballard. "We were kind of on a roll, and when we beat St. Cloud in the WCHA semifinals, it was some of our best hockey of the year. And then we didn't play well at all against Denver. We all knew we had to play better if we were going to go on. I know Adam Berkhoel, one of Denver's goalies, and after they beat us, I told him they could win that one, the regular season and the playoff, but we were going after the big one.

"We knew we had to regroup, to respond to that loss to Denver, to get to the Frozen Four. No matter what we did, we wanted to get that first-round bye. Then all it would take was 60 minutes of hockey and we'd be back at home."

Pohl added that had the Gophers beaten Denver to win the WCHA playoff title, their whole NCAA sequence might have been disrupted. "If we had won that game, we would have had to win something like 12 in a row to win the national title," said Pohl. "I don't know if anybody has done that. And, had we won that Denver game, we probably would have played Michigan in Michigan in the regions. So losing that one got the bad game out of our system, and we were able to focus."

Leopold went back to Game 1. "That first North Dakota game set the whole tone with that third period comeback,' Leo said. "We'd had like, zero before then, a bunch of goose-eggs. We were down 5-1 going into the third against Michigan Tech, and we came back with a tie."

He added that Maine, like Denver, played a pro-style game. "Maine played similar to an AHL team," Leopold said. "Every time they got the puck, they'd flip it up in the air, then hope. We watched tape, and I thought, 'Oh, jeez.' As close as that championship game was, we would have liked to play 'em again. We had a C+ game. We didn't play that well. If that was their best, they outplayed us, and took the game over, but we'd love to play 'em again. I figure their D were out of gas. Metcalf played a lot. We didn't ever have to just stick four guys out there on defense, we could always play our six."

Nick Angell had a special recollection to take away with him: "We opened at North Dakota, and when we won that game 7-5 in their new building. We built on that, but it was still a strange year. We knew we'd be good, coming off making the regionals last year. We hoped we'd be one of the top three or four teams in the league. We knew St. Cloud would be tough, and Colorado College, and we expected North Dakota to be good, because they always are, and Denver kept improving. We were hot at the beginning, then we had a little dip. And then we had that stretch where we couldn't win on Friday nights, but the next game wouldn't even be a game, because we'd dominate so much.

"Then we got going really well at the end of the regular season. We rolled through St. Cloud in the semifinals of the WCHA Final Five, and we knew we were on a roll, and playing great. We said, 'Let's hang a banner,' and that became something of a motto. When we lost to Denver in the WCHA final, we were all disappointed, but looking back now, I really think it helped us. We knew we had been playing great, but then we said, 'We're playing great, but we can't take anything for granted.'

"That helped us the rest of the way. When we beat Maine in overtime, it was a euphoric high. I'll never forget coming out of the locker room, a long time later, and Ben Hankinson was waiting there. He played for the Gophers, of course, and now he's an agent. He was just waiting to congratulate us. He said to me, 'You (bleeping) guys don't even know what you just did. And you won't know until some time down the road, watching somebody else win it on TV.' "

Ben Hankinson played on Gopher teams from 1988-91, and they included a couple of WCHA championship teams, and two final four trips, including the legendary overtime title-game loss to Harvard in 1989 at the Saint Paul Civic Center. Hankinson knows how difficult it is to win an NCAA title, and he knows he never made it. His comment put it best: The 2001-02 Gophers achieved an enormous objective—for themselves, for their fans, and for everybody who ever played for the Gophers in the past, present and future.

Assistant coach Mike Guentzel, who had been with the team for a decade, agreed that nobody could have predicted the outcome, but the potential was there. "The first indication, in hindsight, was how Johnny Pohl and Jordan Leopold took charge, and how hard the team worked through the spring and summer before the season. The guys got along great. There was great chemistry, and we won about half a dozen games where we were behind after two periods.

"You don't realize how many people you touch when you win it," Guentzel added.

Motzko said he realized that all through his first season as the Gophers second assistant. "And after we won, and we were all out on the ice celebrating, I turned to the bench and there's Doug Woog, on the bench, crying," said Motzko. "It was really something to see the people, and all the great feelings from the past, coming back."

Koalska, who is always upbeat and almost invariably greets everybody with a cheerful "Hi, Bud…." or "Hey, how you doin' Bud…." gave a quick assessment of the recent past, the spectacular present and the uncertain future.

"As soon as we lost to Maine last year, we knew we'd be good this year," said Koalska. "We had good guys coming back, and good guys coming in. We had good leadership, from the seniors down. That was good. Every team was tough, and we were struggling so long in the season. But we started getting things together. We've been close all year. We had the guys up to my cabin, up in Detroit Lakes—more by Perham, actually. Got the whole team together. Doesn't matter whether you're a senior or a freshman, we wanted to get the whole team together.

"Denver was a big game. They were really good. It proves you've got to get the bounces. We got 'em. And Denver didn't, against Michigan."

Potulny, always low-key in his analysis, agreed. "Bob Motzko said he'd been involved with teams with more talent that didn't win, and with way less talent that did win," Potulny said. "He thought we had the right mix, the right chemistry. But the best thing that happened to us was losing to Denver. There comes a point where you have to regroup. We hadn't lost for a while, and we had to come back down. We still had two weeks to get ready."

Looking back at the way the Gophers had scrambled to get to their championship peak in the spring of 2002, Potulny said: "There was no time for us to be set up as an NCAA favorite. But we knew we had the potential."

He paraphrased the story assistant coach Motzko had told the team about how much Gopher success meant to all those who had played before. The only nonMinnesotan on the squad, Potulny obviously subscribes to the exact same philosophy of past success. "The way you score goals doesn't matter," Potulny said. "Score as many goals as you want, but in 10 years, when you can hold that ring out, it doesn't matter who was this, who was that, or who scored the goals. It just doesn't matter. It's a team thing. That's all that matters."

While many members of the Gopher team might have scored the winning goal, given the opportunity, nobody questions the obvious fact that Potulny goes to the net and gets his stick on the puck with amazing frequency. His quiet leadership is another asset, and it led to Potulny being named captain of the 2002-03 Gophers, as a junior.

"As for the championship," said Koalska, "some of us may never get a shot at a bigger game. Everybody in Minnesota was probably watching, whether you're a fan or not. This will be something you'll remember forever. You can look back on it when you're 60, sitting on the couch, drinking a Miller High Life.... Obviously, we got back to normal pretty quick. We were working out, knowing it wouldn't be long until we'd be going to school, and it'd be the same old thing.

"But in the back of our heads, we know we won it. After a couple of weeks, you're thinking, 'Let's get the season going again.' It's not going to be any easier for us next year, but we'll be a little more relaxed because we've been there before."

Leopold, who stepped from the ice as an NCAA champion to playing six months later in the NHL with the Calgary Flames, said nothing that any future Gopher team does will alter the accomplishment of the 2002 NCAA championship season.

"I think next year will be more of a rebuilding year," said Leopold. "They should make the NCAAs, but you never know what's going to happen. They'll have some good young talent, but it takes awhile. Maybe when these juniors are seniors, as long as Ballard, Paul Martin and those guys stick around.... But I don't really know what will happen. For the guys coming back, and the incoming freshmen—what can they do? Even if they win it, they can't top what we did, really."

The long and satisfying trip of 2001-02 brought the Golden Gophers back up among the nation's elite college hockey programs. They had returned to their rightful place. Gold Country.

Make that Golden *Gopherhockey* Country.

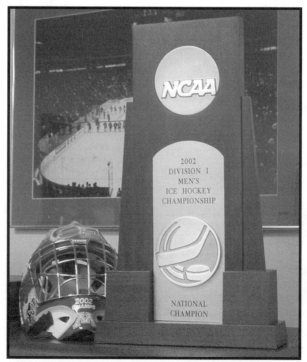

The long-sought trophy for winning the 2002 NCAA national championship sat, temporarily at least, atop a file cabinet in the coaches office at Mariucci Arena. It is the fourth one won by the Golden Gophers, and the first since the Herb Brooks Gophers won titles in 1974, 1976 and 1979.